THE FIRST DAYS OF CLASS

THE FIRST DAYS OF CLASS

A Practical Guide for the Beginning Teacher

Rebecca Lynn Wilke

CORWIN PRESS, INC.
A Sage Publications Company
Thousand Oaks, California

For information:

 Corwin Press, Inc.
A Sage Publications Company
2455 Teller Road
Thousand Oaks, California 91320
www.corwinpress.com

Sage Publications Ltd.
6 Bonhill Street
London EC2A 4PU
United Kingdom

Sage Publications India Pvt. Ltd.
B-42, Panchsheel Enclave
Post Box 4109
New Delhi 110 017 India

Printed in the United States of America

Library of Congress Cataloging-in-Publication Data

Wilke, Rebecca Lynn.
The first days of class: A practical guide for the beginning teacher /
Rebecca Lynn Wilke.
    p. cm.
Includes bibliographical references and index.
ISBN 0-7619-3812-5 (C)— ISBN 0-7619-3813-3 (P)
  1. First year teachers. I. Title.
LB2844.1.N4 W54 2003
371.1—dc21

                          2002010062

This book is printed on acid-free paper.

02 03 04 05 06 10 9 8 7 6 5 4 3 2 1

Acquisitions Editor:	Faye Zucker
Editorial Assistant:	Julia Parnell
Copy Editor:	Teresa Herlinger
Production Editor:	Diane S. Foster
Typesetter:	C&M Digitals (P) Ltd.
Proofreader:	Sally M. Scott
Indexer:	Teri Greenberg
Cover Designer:	Michael Dubowe
Production Artist:	Sandra N. Sauvajot

Contents

Preface

Welcome to the wonderful world of education! The journey ahead of you is full of fantastic opportunities and fun adventures. Although you could have selected numerous career options, I believe that you have chosen the one that will have the greatest impact on society for generations to come. After all, what could be more challenging yet packed with positive potential than working with children?

No matter where you are in the process of becoming a professional in the field of education, you are not alone. Studies show that approximately 200,000 new educators are entering the profession each year, and the demand for qualified teachers to work in today's classrooms continues to increase (Darling-Hammond, Berry, Haselkorn, & Fideler, 1999; Wong & Wong, 1998). Indeed, almost two million teachers will be needed before 2010 (Fideler & Haselkorn, 1999).

As you take your first steps forward in this exciting experience, remember that there are people and resources available to assist you as well. That's what *The First Days of Class: A Practical Guide for the Beginning Teacher* is all about! This book is designed to help you in starting your new career, even if you are the following:

- Beginning your first year of teaching
- Returning to teaching after being out of the field for some time
- Substitute teaching
- Just hired on an emergency contract because of your subject matter expertise
- Considering changing careers
- Working in a practicum at a school site
- In the midst of student teaching
- Finishing your graduate work in education
- Preparing a résumé to send to school districts

- Just entering an education program
- Thinking about becoming a teacher
- Looking for new ideas to improve your classroom instruction as well as make better connections with students' diverse needs
- Mentoring novice teachers to support emerging professionals
- Renewing your own commitment to your profession

After over 14 years in K–12 settings, I am well acquainted with the demands placed on today's educators. We are asked to prepare young people for their futures in a multicultural world where expanding forms of technology will be everyday necessities. In addition, teachers are expected to fill the roles of nurse, counselor, friend, confidant, coach, psychologist, advocate, referee, parent, and much, much more. That's why I've interwoven practical ideas with current educational theory in this easy-to-use guide for exceptional teaching. It is from one educator to another—from someone who has, if you'll excuse the colloquialism, "been there, done that."

The First Days of Class starts by asking you to reflect upon who you are as a person and professional as well as to analyze where you hope to go in this educational experience. There are specific chapters designed to help you create a classroom environment conducive to optimum learning as well as organize and plan your curriculum and instructional methods. Current educational theories on student learning and language and diversity issues are discussed in depth. Most important, *The First Days of Class* will literally walk you though what you can expect during a complete year in the classroom. Whether you are an elementary or secondary school teacher, you will find timeless tips that will help you continue to grow as a professional in the field of education.

As you look at the process involved in becoming an exceptional educator, you may be uncertain of how to even begin. Perhaps this story that Arun Gandhi tells about his famous grandfather will be an encouragement to you. When a would-be protégé came to seek his advice about how to excel in life, Mahatma Gandhi asked an aide to give the young man a bucket and to escort him to the latrines. There he was told to begin cleaning. After several hours, the weary worker returned to Gandhi to ask the purpose of this task. His reply was simple. Before greatness can ever be achieved, one must be willing to start slowly and simply in learning how to serve others. Hopefully you will never have to start your career by cleaning the bathrooms (although I must admit that I've had to supervise restrooms at certain school sites!), but don't expect to start at the top, either. The road to excellence begins right where you are, taking one small step at a time in this wonderful, rewarding career!

Acknowledgments

Many blessings to Nancy Kelly, Dr. Jimmy Phelps, and the myriad of teachers and educators who taught me how to love learning, enjoy life, and, in turn, reach out to others in my world. Your words and wisdom still guide me today, and I'll be forever grateful for being able to spend time with you.

Corwin Press extends its thanks to the following reviewers, whose contributions are gratefully acknowledged:

William Fitzhugh, Reisterstown Elementary School, Reisterstown, MD

Brenda Hartshorn, Moretown Elementary School, Moretown, VT

Steve Hutton, Beechwood Elementary School, Ft. Mitchell, KY

Kenneth Klopack, Funston Elementary School, Chicago, IL

Bonnie Watson, Owensboro Middle School, Owensboro KY.

Wanted

Men and women with the patience of Job, the wisdom of Solomon, and the ability to prepare the next generation for productive citizenship under highly adverse and sometimes dangerous conditions. Applicants must be willing to fill gaps left by unfit, absent, or working parents, satisfy demands of state politicians and local bureaucrats, impart healthy cultural and moral values and—oh yes—teach the three R's. Hours: 50-60 per week. Pay: Fair (getting better!). Rewards: mostly intangible.

—Anonymous

About the Author

Rebecca Lynn Wilke, Ed.D., is a university professor as well as an educational and leadership consultant. Dr. Wilke has worked with children and adults of all ages in public and private school settings for over 20 years. In addition, she and her husband, Dr. Steve Wilke, operate LEADon, Inc., an organization dedicated to transforming the personal and professional lives of corporate leaders across America. They provide pre-employment assessment, executive coaching, high-performance team building, group training, and leadership evaluations for everyone from interns to executives.

Dr. Wilke is a graduate of the University of Southern California where she specialized in Educational Leadership and Multicultural Education. She can be reached on the World Wide Web at Leadon.biz or via e-mail at Doctorswilke@cox.net.

Dedicated to my family, whose love and encouragement always allowed me to dream about life's possibilities! My husband, Steve—thank you for all the support and devotion that you've shown over the years—you have always been my biggest fan. My boys, Ryan and Jared—you taught me what is best about being a mom. My treasured friends—Teri, Laura, Tammy, Heather, "et al."—who have shared life's journey with me and made it much more joyous! And, most important, to a gracious God who is my center each day and great hope for tomorrow.

1

Getting Ready to Interview

Personal Reflection, Picking the Right Path, and Interview Readiness

In a completely rational society, the best of us would aspire to be teachers and the rest of us would have to settle for something less, because passing civilization along from one generation to the next ought to be the highest honor and the highest responsibility anyone could have.

—Lee Iacocca

" I want my résumé to be the one you remember. It's also available as a music video, interpretive dance, and a haiku."

After much time, thought, and effort, you are ready to begin a new, exciting career. Perhaps you have longed for this type of position for years, or maybe the yearning to work with young people is relatively new. Wherever you are on this journey toward becoming a teacher, it is essential that you take some time to reflect upon what you've done to reach this place in life and how you'd like to see yourself develop as a professional in the days, weeks, and years ahead of you.

After finishing your education courses as well as the practicum and student teaching experiences, you may still feel unprepared to be in charge of your own classroom. You know that you've done a tremendous amount of work to get ready for this adventure, but you're uncertain about how you'll be as a leader. Don't worry; you are not alone in these concerns. Most individuals who have entered the field of education have experienced similar apprehension. Remember, some anxiety can be a plus because it encourages all of us to grow and stretch in areas that we might normally tend to avoid.

Once you have been hired for a particular position, you will have much to accomplish before you embark upon the actual work of teaching young people. Although this process is seldom discussed in education courses due to time constraints, I believe the most essential "first step," before you even interview for a teaching job, is to spend several hours reflecting upon who you are as an individual and professional. Without being fully aware of your own strengths and weaknesses, you will more than likely struggle in some significant ways during the early part of your new career.

Here's an analogy that should help you understand this point. Before expert backpackers set out on a hike, they take an in-depth analysis of the trip that they are about to undertake. Based upon the path to be traveled, they assess their own abilities to reach the end successfully. If one of the hikers has a weak ankle, he or she will wear certain shoes and pack equipment accordingly. If another of the adventurers tends to get dehydrated, he'll pack extra water. If the sun will be out, those with sensitive skin will generously apply sunscreen.

No matter how many trips these backpackers have made in the past, they will spend time assessing their strengths and weaknesses for this particular journey. How about you? How prepared are you for this new venture in life? Is your résumé in good shape? Have you reviewed the types of questions that might be asked during an interview? Do you know what your abilities are? And what about the more personal aspects of who you are? Are you aware of how your upbringing, culture, and community play a role in how you interact with others? All of these essential aspects make up the real "you" and, most important, will impact how you relate to the students that will be part of your classroom.

#1

TEACHER, KNOW THYSELF

An accurate assessment of who we are as individuals is rarely ever done in life, especially when we're about to start a new career! One of the main reasons is time. Most of us are so busy living life that we don't have any spare minutes left over for self-reflection and analysis. In addition, you have been focused on completing all of the requirements to attain your teaching credential as well as a position; it is a miracle that you still have energy left over to read this book! Don't stress if you feel that this is one more thing to add to your "to do" list. The advice that I'm offering should be painless, and the effort that you invest in these endeavors now will benefit you greatly in the days ahead.

Reflection

Part of this self-assessment process will involve stretching and struggling in areas that you may not have experienced before, and the best of our seasoned educators will tell you that an important aspect of this involves interpersonal experiences and self-reflection. Spending time now understanding more about who you are as an individual will not only help you become a better person, but it will also aide in your development as a professional. And, as I can tell you from my own experiences, it will help you avoid mistakes as you relate to students, parents, and co-workers down the road.

As you begin to reflect, try to remember what it was like for you when you were growing up. Where did you live during your first ten years of life? What was the community and culture like? Who were your main caregivers? What type of values did your parents, grandparents, teachers, and even community members try to instill in you?

Learning Preferences

I'd also like you to consider the style of learning that you experienced when you went to elementary school. Were there certain teachers who impacted you more than others? Which ones, and why? The reason that I ask this is that many educators enter this profession because of a particular teacher (or teachers) who greatly influenced their lives. Often, we will find that our own philosophy of education or style of instruction may reflect these influences in our development.

Spend some time thinking about the way that you tend to learn new information. For example, are you a visual learner? Do you prefer to see something written down or in picture form before someone tells you about it? If you are the type who likes to read the instruction manual before you program the VCR, you are probably a visual person. Or do you need new data explained to you? People who enjoy listening to the radio, cassettes, and CDs are often auditory learners. There are some individuals who are more "hands-on," which educational experts would call kinesthetic learners. You would rather take something apart, then put it back together again by yourself. Reading a manual or having someone talk you through the job would be a waste of time, since you learn by doing.

Once you have identified which of the three types of learners you are—*visual, auditory, or kinesthetic*—you will begin to understand why you typically develop your lesson plans the way you do. While it is beneficial for you to work within your area of expertise and comfort, you also need to be aware that this may be a mismatch for some of your students. If you are an auditory person, and you give most of your class directions orally, the visual learners can easily become lost in the process. If you always make presentations with overheads or use the lecture method, those students who learn better by doing will become bored and, possibly, unruly.

Multiple Intelligences

The style in which you or your students learn is only one of the educational considerations that must be understood when we discuss how people acquire and process information. Another recent theory developed by a professor from Harvard University is that of multiple intelligences. Dr. Howard Gardner contends that there are many areas of intelligence and that learners can be "gifted" in one or more of these main categories: mathematical-logical, linguistic, spatial, musical, bodily-kinesthetic, interpersonal, and intra-personal intelligences. Recent investigations suggest that emotional, naturalistic, and existential intelligence could be added to this list (Gardner, 2000). A wonderful resource for teachers by Thomas Armstrong is *Multiple Intelligences in the Classroom* (Armstrong, 2000; see Resource B, Recommended Reading). This book will not only allow you to analyze your own strengths and weaknesses, but it will also help you gather ideas on how to fully address the giftedness in all of your students.

Cultural Heritage and Diversity

Another personal assessment to undertake before you actually begin teaching involves reflecting on your own culture, ethnicity, and family heritage. I believe that this will be an unusual and perhaps daunting task for many of us. While some families may have lost part of their cultural identity because of the "melting pot" philosophy that has been prevalent in the United States for decades, many individuals and ethnic groups are now attempting to get in touch with their cultural roots. This may involve talking to grandparents or other members of the family, or you may have to investigate old family albums and genealogy records. Knowing our cultural heritage is essential to having a strong sense of who we are as individuals.

Realize that all cultural influences play a part in what makes you unique as well as how you approach others. The only reason that other people's practices seem unusual to us is that we often compare them to our own! *When you accept the distinctive qualities of your background, ethnicity, language, and heritage, you will be much more open and accepting of the cultural differences of others.*

As most of us are aware, the demographics of our student population have changed dramatically in the United States during the past several decades. This is also true in many other industrialized nations around the globe. In numerous cities across America, the "minority" groups have become the majority, so it is essential that today's teachers not only understand about culture but also create positive connections with students from diverse backgrounds (Darling-Hammond et al., 1999; Garcia, 1994). If you are interested in learning more about diversity as well as finding ways to educate children from a multicultural perspective, I suggest reading Dr. James Banks' text *Multiethnic Education: Theory and Practice* (Banks, 1994; see Resource B, Recommended Reading). As you delve deeper into these issues, you will be better prepared to work with the diverse students who will comprise your classroom. (We'll look at this topic in more detail in Chapter 5.)

PROFESSIONALISM   #2

In addition to reflecting upon your own background and culture, you should begin to visualize yourself as a professional in the field of education. Although you may be leaving the university, a business position, the military, or some other occupation to become a teacher, this new position will have its own particular demands. Indeed, the complex and multifaceted tasks that most educators balance on a daily basis are more than many doctors, lawyers, or engineers would be willing to handle!

Beware of Cynicism!

Even though teaching is highly valued by many in our society, unfortunately, there will be some negative forces that you will have to confront as you journey through your career. Plenty of people will cross your path who may try to devalue your new profession; you may have already met some of them during your college experience. They say things like, "You want to be a teacher? What for?" or, "Of all the jobs that you could have picked, you want to work with lots of kids for little money?" It's hard to smile in the face of such cynicism, although you can let these doubters know that teacher salaries have been on a steady increase since the 1990s (NCES Digest of Education Statistics, 1999). Besides, no amount of money can compare to the benefit of helping young people succeed in life. Many people who are not part of this wonderful profession will never understand that fact!

Confidence

An enormous struggle for new teachers is cultivating the confidence needed in this challenging career. Every novice employee has these same feelings to some degree, but not everyone will have to face thirty or more inquisitive faces each morning that may also be wondering if you're good enough for this position. If the kids aren't thinking this, then their parents probably are! Self-confidence is essential from the very beginning. You have selected this career because you enjoy it, and obviously you have the skills and expertise in your subject area or you wouldn't have received a credential. Recognize your assets and abilities, and regularly remind yourself of them when you start to feel a little shaky. (This is one good reason to hang your diplomas, credentials, and other documents in your classroom; sometimes you need a visible reminder of just how far you've come in life!)

I'll be the first to admit to you that teaching isn't easy. Today's educators must be knowledgeable in numerous areas as well as be able to relate information at a moment's notice. There is also an enormous amount of pressure placed upon teachers regarding pupil performance, test scores, and preparation as citizens of the future. You will have many more responsibilities than Plato ever dreamed of when he taught in the "outdoor school" centuries ago (Lee, 1987).

COMMITMENT   #3

Another vital aspect of teaching is that you must truly love the job that you do. Sure, there will be days when you wish that you had chosen dentistry or interior design, but overall you should find pleasure in the mere fact that you get to work with kids. After all, they truly are our national treasures! Though young people can be trying at times (especially when they can't seem to sit still), for the most part they are willing to adapt to anything you want them to do. Students almost innately want to please and perform for their teachers, so gain their respect early on and you'll be able to accomplish great things!

You have probably known a teacher who didn't like his or her job. This is tragic, because the students are usually well aware of these feelings. Some people entered this profession merely to have a "secure" position that paid decently. Others may have been highly motivated when they started teaching, but somewhere along the road they "burned out" and couldn't (or wouldn't) leave. *Don't let this happen to you!* If you are already wondering whether or not this is the right job for you, then spend more time pondering your career choice. If you are questioning your commitment to this profession now, you may grow to hate it down the road. Sadly, that's when both you and the students will suffer.

You will never regret setting aside a weekend or several quiet afternoons in order to think about some of the questions and concepts in this chapter. After some self-analysis, you will not only be more aware of who you are as a person and professional, but you will also be more certain of how your life experiences will affect your relationship with your students. Resolve to spend quality time reflecting on these ideas so that you can take the next important steps toward becoming an exceptional teacher.

PLANNING YOUR PATH

Life usually leads us down a variety of paths. Sometimes the route we take is smooth and clearly marked, while at other times things get a bit bumpy—and we may even reach a fork in the road from time to time. You may have been on a different course in life before you decided to investigate a career in education, but now you know what direction you're headed, and you can't wait to get there!

School Settings

As you think about your potential teaching position, you may have some questions about your final destination. Often new educators don't realize that there are different options available to them. Sometimes there is so much pressure to find a job—any job—that little forethought is given as to exactly where you'd like to spend the next decade, or two—or three—of your life! Statistics show that once a teacher commits to a particular district, he or she is less likely to move elsewhere (National Center for Education Statistics, 1999). Therefore, take some time before you sign that contract to figure out exactly where you'd like to invest your time, effort, and energy during the years ahead.

Although we could spend several chapters talking about the different types of schools across the United States, suffice it to say that you have three major options: public, private, and parochial school settings. Each of these will offer you many opportunities to fulfill your dreams of working with young people, but you will have to be the one to figure out which type of climate and culture is right for you.

Public Schools

Public schools have a rich history in the United States; their development has directly corresponded to the transition of the American people and their needs during the past four centuries (Johnson, Dupuis, Musial, Hall, & Gollnick, 2002; Shatzer, 1999). Public school environments are based on concepts like "education for all" and how to produce "philosopher kings" from ordinary citizens (Johnson et al., 2002; Lee, 1987; Spring, 1998). Although the burgeoning size of public schools can be overwhelming for some, the multitude of opportunities for up-to-date resources, access to technology, and professional growth are unparalleled.

Private Schools

Out of approximately 53 million school children in the United States, 5.9 million of these attend private schools (National Association of Independent Schools, October 2000). Private settings are typically smaller than most public institutions, and the student/teacher ratio tends to be low. Parent involvement is usually high, but salaries often cannot compete with the tax-dollar supported schools. Parochial schools are private schools that are run by a parish, church, or religious group. Like private schools, they operate from their own independent philosophies, but the First Amendment prevents federal money from going directly to teacher salaries (Johnson et al., 2002; Spring, 1998).

Due to societal changes, some students, parents, and educators feel safer and more able to express their personal and religious beliefs in private or parochial school settings (National Center for Education Statistics, 1999; Shatzer, 1999), but we have also seen tremendous reform efforts being made in all areas of public education (Darling-Hammond, 1997; Fullan, 1993; Spring, 1998). The most important thing to remember is that all of these institutions are in business for one reason: to benefit the lives of all students. Whether it is teaching the "3 R's" or developing character in the lives of young people, these schools are striving to make society a better place for all of us (DeRoche & Williams, 2001). So, spend some time evaluating what type of educational setting would be best for your skills, philosophy, and style.

THE NUTS AND BOLTS OF INTERVIEW PREPARATION

Now that you've done a thorough self-assessment, including asking yourself what type of school setting would suit you best, you're ready to interview for your first teaching position—well, almost. There's a little more prep work to do. But after all that soul searching, this should be a snap. The first task is to make sure your paperwork is in proper order. Most important, make certain that all of the requirements for the placement file kept at your university are met. Someone in the school of education can review the file (whether it is an open or closed one) and inform you of any other documents that you may need to include now or at some future date. Remember that you will want to include letters of reference to this file as you gain experience in the field of education (and be sure to keep copies of any letters that principals, fellow teachers, parents, and other professionals provide you for your personal records at home).

A second step toward preparing for your new position is to create a professional résumé. This French term literally translates "to summarize." Although synthesizing one's life onto a single sheet may seem impossible, it is a key document to keep up-to-date throughout your career. Résumé formats and styles do vary, but most should include these main ingredients:

❖   ❖   ❖

Core Content of Your Résumé

1. Vital statistics: Name, address, e-mail, phone, and fax numbers

2. Job objective: List specifics according to the position

3. Education: List college(s) attended, degree(s) attained, years of attendance

4. Work experience: Include positions related to teaching, but any job that shows you were a responsible employee is important

5. Certification: List your state certification document(s) along with any other specific licenses or credentials that you may hold

6. Honors/Awards: Include a few achievements that will provide insight into your capabilities as well as extracurricular activities

7. Professional Organizations/Community Involvement: Provide examples from both inside and outside the educational arena

8. References: Often "available upon request" is sufficient, but a brief list of people along with their addresses can be given *as long as they have given you permission to do so*

❖ ❖ ❖

Remember, a résumé is a brief snapshot of who you are. Make sure that it is clear, concise, and professional. This might be *the* document that encourages someone to call you in for an interview. If you are overwhelmed by the task of developing your own résumé, there are individuals and businesses that specialize in these services. Also, many educators are choosing to post their résumés online for prospective employers. As time goes by, you will want to add updated information to your résumé so that it will be a handy resource for future professional contacts.

Another tool that is highly recommended by experts in the field of education is the Professional Teaching Portfolio (Jensen & Kiley, 2000). This is a compilation of documents and materials that showcases your strengths, qualifications, and ongoing development in the field of education. This portfolio should be a "work in progress," and it can actually be started during the student teaching experience. Sample lessons, work done by students,

---

Box 1.1

REHEARSING FOR A TEACHING INTERVIEW

Potential Interview Questions

1. Tell us about yourself.

2. Why did you decide to become a teacher?

3. Describe your educational background for me.

4. What kind of experiences have you had in the field of education?

5. Can you define your philosophy of education?

6. Explain how you think you will fit into this position.

7. How do you best work with other people?

8. What will your classroom management be like? (They may give you an actual scenario and ask how you would solve it.)

9. What professional organizations do you belong to? Do you read certain educational journals?

10. What books or people have had most impact on your life?

11. In what ways would you be an asset to our school?

12. Where do you see yourself in five (ten) years?

13. What are your strengths? Weaknesses?

14. How do you plan to keep in touch with parents?

15. What will you do to keep current in the field of education? In your content area?

16. Are there any questions that you'd like to ask us?

---

photographs of activities, and even a video tape of your teaching can be included in this montage of your mounting educational experiences. You might put together a binder, flexible file folder, or some other compact, easily transportable form to organize the portfolio work.

Finally, as you reflect upon your preparation for teaching, how confident do you feel about what will be asked of you by potential employers? The interview process is a component of any job search, but the questions that future teachers are typically asked are often highly specific and unique to the field of education. When you are called to an interview, be sure that you have these details down on paper:

❖   ❖   ❖

Core Questions for Your Teaching Interview

1. When is the interview?

2. Where will it be? (I recommend that you drive to this site a day in advance to become familiar with your surroundings as well as have the opportunity to study the culture and climate of the community before the interview.)

3. Who (and how many) will be involved in the interviewing process? (Find out specific names with correct spellings so that you can send thank-you notes later. Please be aware that there are often teams of people who assist with interviews for prospective teachers.)

4. What specific position will you be interviewing for? (This information will help you prepare for potential questions that you will be asked.)

5. What will the process involve? (Will you need to make time to fill out paperwork or write a short essay? Should you bring your career portfolio along?)

❖   ❖   ❖

Of course you'll want to put your best foot forward during the interviewing process. Prepare an appropriate outfit in advance, and make sure it is clean and pressed ahead of time. Although everyone's idea of "appropriate" attire may vary, think about what you would wear to any *professional* engagement. If you aren't certain, ask a friend or family member for help. This person would also be a good resource to assist you in preparing for the actual interview. Some sample questions are provided in Box 1.1. Practice them until you feel comfortable with your answers. As you do so, you will gain more confidence in your ever-expanding role as an educator.

Tips to Remember

1. Mark a day in your calendar that will be spent thinking about the contents of this chapter. Call it your "Who Am I?" day.

2. Make sure your placement file, résumé, and career portfolio are in good shape. Photocopy letters of reference and other important documents (like applications sent to school districts) for your own records at home.

3. Spend time rehearsing potential interview questions with a friend so that you feel confident about your ideas on educating young people.

4. Write down what countries your ancestors came from. How do you think these cultures impact the things that you do today?

5. Order a book on learning styles or multicultural education so that you can study these educational issues before the first day of school.

2

Where It All Happens

Creating the Right Atmosphere

Never lose an opportunity of seeing any that is beautiful; for beauty is God's handwriting—a wayside sacrament. Welcome it in every fair face, in every fair sky, in every fair flower, and thank God for it as a cup of blessing.

—Ralph Waldo Emerson

"Home schooling isn't as great as I thought it would be. For Chemistry class, I have to test the chemical reaction between liquid soap and a pile of dirty dishes. For Math, I have to subtract dirt from the carpet and add polish to the furniture. For Phys Ed, it's a grueling lawn care triathlon. ..."

After much toil, and sometimes tribulation, you've finally attained the title of teacher. With the position will come rights and responsibilities. In addition, you will also have the pleasure of establishing an environment where enormous amounts of learning will take place. Whether your assigned classroom is old or new, low tech or high tech, it is basically yours to design, decorate, and do with as you please. As you start to contemplate this new setting, you will have more concerns than simple placement of chairs, cabinets, and desks. You will also take on the issues and concerns of an established organization with its specific culture and climate. The choices you make at this juncture will start to shape your professional life just as you are helping to shape the lives of your students.

SCHOOL CULTURE

No doubt you remember stepping onto various campuses during your practicum and student teaching experiences and realizing that each one had its own unique "feel." Although hard to pin down at times, you could sense a happy spirit at some schools, while other settings seemed more serious or even glum. There are certain institutions that seem just like the name—almost factory-like in appearance—with large, unwelcoming fences guarding their extremities. Yet there are other places that have "curb appeal"; the green grass, shade trees, and bright flowers around the flagpole make you want to stop by and stay awhile. Even the secretary's kind smile at some sites makes you feel like you've come home after a long journey.

What I'm describing is the actual culture on school campuses. Each educational institution has one, although the staff and students are sometimes oblivious to this fact. Yet every organization has its own unique way of integrating human behavior, transmitting knowledge, interacting inside and outside of the company, and communicating (Deal & Kennedy, 1982). Environment is just one aspect of culture. A school's culture is also seen in its values, heroes, rites, and rituals, as well as its "culture bearers." These culture bearers are typically the leaders in the group who feel compelled to pass on the structure of the culture to the next generation. In educational settings, these people would include the experienced teachers on campus as well as some members of the administration and supporting staff. As a new educator at your site, it will be vital that you take an accurate assessment of the intricacies and idiosyncrasies of your particular school's climate and culture, for by doing so you will adjust and become part of the team more easily.

Many aspects of the culture of schools are positive: the good feel they give us when we go to work (your students will feel this, too); the positive, "can-do" spirit, and the forgiving nature when mistakes are made. But sometimes these elements are missing, or there may be other negative aspects of culture that we'd like to cure: negativism, unkindness, even hostility. And, despite many efforts at reform, educational experts will tell you that the core culture of teaching and learning is difficult to change—as is true of any old, established institution (Fullan, 1993).

What I recommend is that you begin your teaching career with an understanding that the school where you will be working is not perfect—and never will be. It is made up of humans, and, as we know, we are all flawed. The good news is this place will have many wonderful qualities that will make your job and the learning opportunities for your students both positive and powerful. Look for these promising characteristics of your school's culture early on, and find out who the key players are that are positively impacting the lives of students. Learn how you can fit into your new environment best, and, over time, you will be able to help mold your school's method of passing on learning to the next generation.

DEFINING YOUR NEW SPACE

Student Desks

As you begin to look at the layout of your new classroom, the seating arrangements of the students should be foremost in your mind. Their ability to see the board and/or your primary area of teaching should be analyzed from every angle before you begin placing chairs and desks. Although it is beneficial to completely clear out a room as you begin this process, in some situations this is impossible. For example, a physics or biology lab usually has permanent workstations, so you will have to develop your plan around these structures. If you can't manipulate the furnishings very easily, then it may be best to draw several rough sketches of the space with different designs that you think will work. Be sure to enlist the assistance of the custodian(s) before attempting to move anything that's large or heavy. You don't want to be injured before your job actually begins!

A desired quality of most classroom designs is that they can be changed over time. You may discover that what you had thought would be a perfect plan at the start of the school year simply won't work for second graders, or the circle formation allows too much "visiting" time for middle schoolers. The main idea is to keep the environment focused on the reason that the kids are there—to acquire information in the easiest manner possible!

Space to Move Around

The *ideal* classroom will have extra work and storage spaces that can be accessed easily and allow everyone to move around comfortably. Notice the emphasis on ideal. Even though you may wish for a roomy environment, the reality is that many classes are cramped—and once the children arrive, they become even more crowded. It is essential that your students don't feel claustrophobic in a place where they are going to spend many hours of their day. You may have to consider grouping desks together or removing a large table that, although handy, simply takes up too much room.

Teacher's Desk

The placement of the teacher's desk is a personal choice. Some educators like this area to have a central location so it is accessible to the students. Other teachers feel that the student desks and chairs should take center stage, so they put their workstation in a corner or in the back of the classroom. The decision is entirely yours, but do remember that this space is important since you will probably keep grades, teacher texts, and other sensitive materials on hand. Establishing proper boundaries for your work area will be vital information to give your students on the first day of school.

WORKING WONDERS WITH WALLS

By now you will have spent a great deal of time observing and working in other classrooms. No doubt you noticed the wide variety of decorating methods that educators employ. Some like the learning environment to be simple; they would heartily agree with the adage "less is more." You may think that other teachers studied at LeRoy Neiman's school of art because of the bright, bold colors and vivid artistry that adorn every inch of wall space.

Although the actual interior design of the classroom is up to you, once again you need to keep your students in mind. They should feel comfortable in the creative confines of your classroom. Everything from color to contact paper can impact students, especially those who are "visual learners." Think about what things you can do to accentuate your space without causing overstimulation.

Color

As I mentioned, some things can't be changed in your room. Paint color is an obvious one. Fortunately, many sites have moved away from "institution green," but the basic beige or peeling peach may not be to your liking. The best suggestion I can make is to cover up what isn't pleasing to the eye with interesting posters, banners, quilts, or even framed artwork. Hopefully, a few years down the line, you'll be in a tenured position where you can request some changes that fit into the school budget. Be patient, though. Once I worked in a classroom that was long overdue for painting. A year after my formal request, the money was finally budgeted, but, due to misplaced paperwork, the workmen almost skipped my room. Fortunately, I followed the paper trail and was able to get things back on track. Being persistent is another plus in this career!

Wall Art

As a beginning teacher, you may find that you don't have the funds for the fabulous decorations that you see in teacher supply stores and catalogs. That's okay! I recommend that you purchase a small supply of the materials that you'll use over and over again. For example, a math teacher would want to have a chart of the multiplication tables. If you teach English, look for posters of classic novels or pictures of landscapes and scenic settings for story prompts. You can also make interesting wall art on your own, like a huge tree out of crepe paper or mural-size collages from magazines and catalogs. Collect old calendars and magazines from friends and neighbors to make a colorful bulletin board. Parents are often willing to bring in used copies of *National Geographic, Time,* or trade journals. Don't be shy about asking around campus either. Seasoned teachers often have drawers— even closets—full of materials that may help add color and creativity to your classroom.

Bulletin Boards

Realize that this space belongs to your students as well. Adding things that they enjoy will only increase their pleasure in coming to your room each day. All kids love to see their own work along with that of their fellow students, so be sure to have at least one bulletin board or wall dedicated to their master-pieces. Be sure to update this area regularly, so that each new, innovative activity is displayed for the benefit of students, parents, and administrators. You may even set up a system where the students get to change a wall space or board once a month. This is another excellent way to get them involved in the learning process!

SETTING THE TONE

You know how comforting it is to turn the key in the latch and enter your home at the end of a long day. As you step inside, the pains and problems that bothered you a few minutes before seem to slip away in the soothing surroundings of your own personal space. This is the type of sensation that you should try to create in your new work environment. When you enter the classroom, there should be sights, smells, and sounds that prompt pleasant feelings and make you want to stay awhile. As educational experts point out, the overall classroom environment truly impacts how students and teachers feel (Weinstein, 1996).

Classrooms don't have to be clean and efficient, like hospital emergency rooms. How about creating an environment that makes everyone want to come in, curl up with a good book (or whatever lesson you've got planned for that day), and visit with you for a spell? Here are a few ideas to think about for your new space:

❖   ❖   ❖

Creating Your Classroom Space

- Place plants and even a tree in the room to bring a more natural touch.
- Make a cozy reading corner with a comfy chair and throw pillows on the floor.
- Purchase an old lamp at a yard sale or bargain store to add softer lighting at the art table or study corral.
- Bring in your stereo from home to play anything from classical to contemporary songs. If the students are not thrilled with your choice in music, then give them times to listen to their favorite radio station, or bring in tapes or CDs on certain days of the week.

❖   ❖   ❖

Your classroom is truly a place where living as well as learning will occur. Both you and your students will be spending precious minutes, hours, and days of your lives in this space, so have fun creating a special setting that everyone will enjoy! As you begin the school year, you may find that there are things that you need to change, or the kids (or you) might become bored with the arrangement and need something new. Then go ahead—redecorate! The more pleasing and pleasant the classroom environment is, the more you'll like what you're doing—and the students will, too!

Tips to Remember

1. Over the next few months, make notes in a journal about your school's culture. Keep track of its unique character-istics. Who are the "culture bearers"? Most important, write down ideas on how you see yourself fitting into the new community. In what areas would you like to experi-ence personal and professional growth?

2. Make some drawings of your new classroom. Sketch out different design possibilities that you'd like to try during the school year, and be sure to keep these in a file folder for future use.

3. If you travel from class to class, or share a room with another teacher, you may have to wait a year or two to really test out your own designs. Use this time to study what other teachers are doing, and make notes for future reference of what you'd like to try.

4. Ask other teachers, art stores, or the school librarian for wall decorations that they may not use or want any longer. Let friends and family know what you need for your class so they can help keep an eye out for these types of materials.

5. Before doing anything permanent, always check with an administrator. Many school districts have specific codes or restrictions for the health and safety of both students and staff.

3

So Much to Do, So Little Time

How Do You Organize It All?

Before beginning, prepare carefully.

—Cicero

GLASBERGEN

**"Before we begin our Time Management Seminar,
did everyone get one of these 36-hour wrist watches?"**

L earning to organize all of the materials and information required in a new position can be an overwhelming task for any professional. For teachers, this is especially true because of the limitations of the school schedule. Whether you are compulsively neat and tidy or typically relaxed in your organizational style, it is a good idea to take some time to analyze all of the requirements and expectations of your new job. As you begin the process of teaching, you'll greatly benefit from starting out with the most efficient system possible to make your experience in the classroom and with your students as carefree as possible.

ANALYZING YOUR ORGANIZATIONAL STYLE

All of us have our own ideas and *ideals* about how life should be arranged and organized. As you have experienced during your practicum and student teaching, each educator seems to have a system that works best for him or her. Some professionals are perfectionists by nature; in their classes, everything has a specifically allotted space. In fact, items are probably labeled and lined up in alphabetical order! Other teachers find that a casual method of cataloging meets their needs, although they'd probably tell you that their peers say they're in a state of working chaos!

No matter what method seasoned professionals may use in the classroom, they will attest to the fact that you must establish a style for keeping the curriculum, materials, and class records in working order. Based on years of teaching experience in all types of classrooms, I can tell you that it will be beneficial to start this system early on in your career. The positive habits and patterns that you establish now will assure your success in the future.

KEEPING THE CURRICULUM GOING

I believe that an essential step toward great teaching is having an established plan and purpose for the educational process. Remember, curriculum involves *what* you will teach the students. This includes the course requirements, textbooks, and other materials that must be covered before the students move on to the next level, class, or grade. If you don't start the school year with some

what is the pace?

idea of what should be covered during that month, semester, and year, you could end up only halfway through the math book in May, wondering how to cover six more chapters in three weeks' time! (There will be additional advice on how to organize your curriculum in Chapter 6.)

Preparing Your Curriculum Calendar

As you look forward to the first day of the new semester, I suggest that you sit down with a calendar in one hand and your curriculum guide in the other to do your long-range planning. If you haven't familiarized yourself with the text and other materials to be covered in your class(es), this is an ideal time to do so. It may take many hours, even days, of dedication, but it will be time well spent. Once the students arrive, you will encounter many distractions that will deter you from doing an in-depth analysis of the curriculum.

Content Goals

While you are studying these materials, make notes on the calendar of goals and deadlines that you need to meet. In other words, if the U.S. History textbook is 12 chapters long, you would certainly want to have completed Chapter 6 by the end of the first semester. If you're teaching a third-grade spelling program, you should check when the mandated testing will occur in order to plan for completion of the unit by this date. Perhaps your district requires that students in English classes read one novel per month. It would be important to note this on your working calendar.

Test Dates

Standardized testing has become a critical component of the educational process during the last decade. This is partly due to accountability issues as educational institutions attempt to make positive changes and reforms (Fullan, 1993; Spring, 1998). These testing dates are usually posted on the master calendar for your school; this is also where you can locate other scheduled events that you should post on your own working calendar. Check with your school's secretary for a copy of this schedule if one has not been placed in your mailbox.

Sharing Schedules With Colleagues

It is also a good idea to discover what other teachers in your school are doing in terms of scheduling. Many schools now group teachers in teams so they can brainstorm ideas and work together with the same group of children. In these instances, it will be essential to do short- and long-term planning with your co-workers. Even if you work in a large setting within a department of educators, you can ask that suggestions on the curriculum be discussed as well as the pacing of units. Many teachers are happy to share materials and ideas, and, down the road, you will have the wonderful opportunity of passing on your own teacher-developed activities and lessons to others.

Expecting the Unexpected

Obviously, you will want to keep your calendar in close proximity to the workstation where you will do your day-to-day planning, and be sure to check it each week. Once the school year begins, you'll need to be flexible about the dates you've selected for various objectives. Many things seem to creep into our schedules—special assemblies, fire drills, last-minute teacher workdays, surprise guest speakers, and so forth. You might also discover that you didn't allot enough time for a particular unit one month, but you overestimated the following section by two weeks. Don't panic! Every teacher has to learn the art of give and take when it comes to scheduling. In the end, everything should work out well as long as you've started with a systemized plan of attack.

MANAGING MATERIALS

Educators have a myriad of materials they must utilize while working with students, many of which depend on the subject area and grade levels that are taught. For physical education personnel, these include balls, bats, jump ropes, cones, clipboards, and even whistles. Teachers assigned to elementary schools use everything from glue to Gummy Bears, crayons to activity centers, and Dr. Seuss books to building blocks. Science teachers have highly sensitive chemicals that must be carefully controlled, while art instructors must keep track of expensive supplies.

Your Supply List

As you begin to assess your curriculum, make a list of any items you will need to start the school year. Be sure to inform your principal or department chairperson about what you feel is essential for your course(s). The school should provide you with most materials that you need. Basic items are usually taken care of soon after you turn in a detailed list to the person in charge of supplies, but some things you will simply have to purchase on your own. Schools have an annual budget with a certain amount set aside for teaching materials (although new teachers often receive a little extra to help get them started). It is essential that you learn to operate within your budget in order to show the administration that you have already mastered this important organizational skill!

Making Order and Consistency Contagious

As you gather the equipment and other supplies that you will use this year, start organizing them in your room. Books, classroom kits, manipulatives, art supplies, and items for projects and activities are just some of the tools of the trade that you will want to have handy. If your materials are misplaced or get out of order, they can be hard to find and use when you need them most. Begin by selecting a place for special supplies, like teacher textbooks and easily damaged items, that only you should have access to—perhaps behind or near your desk or workstation. Certain resources, like dictionaries or encyclopedias, should be placed where they are readily available to the students.

Small items can easily get lost in the everyday shuffle of school life. I used to purchase a variety of storage materials—everything from plastic bags to larger storage tubs—to stow away things like scissors, math manipulatives, flashcards, games, and art supplies. Be sure to label these containers with a dark, permanent marker. On the first day of school, you should instruct your students about where you'd like these materials to be kept in the classroom and in what condition you expect to find them after they've been used. Although your students may argue that another teacher does things differently, patiently explain to them that this is how *you* want these class supplies to be treated all year long. Once an organized system has been established, the chances that you'll have most or all of these items at the end of the school year will be greatly increased, and you'll have less of these products to purchase for the upcoming year. In addition, order and consistency are often contagious—and this is definitely something you'd like your students to catch!

DOCUMENTATION

Creating Your Filing System

Most professionals have some sort of filing system where they keep pertinent records and important documentation. As a new teacher, this is a crucial part of the organizational design that you will need to create. As busy as you will soon be, you must have your files arranged to enable immediate access to them—such as in a locking file cabinet near your desk. With all the events that take place during the school day, only someone with a photographic memory could recall dates and details of things like parent phone calls, discipline procedures, or the latest staff meeting highlights. Buy a big box of file folders now and label them with categories such as the following:

ESSENTIAL FILE FOLDERS

1. Meetings (you might want a separate folder for each type that you attend, for example, Faculty Minutes, Department Updates, or IEP Meetings)

2. Parent Contacts

3. Counseling Referrals

4. Disciplinary Action (detentions, referrals, or suspensions)

5. Lesson Plans (themes, units, or specific lessons, for example, Nutrition, Phonics, Shakespeare, Volleyball)

6. Grades (past quarter, trimester, etc.)

7. School Procedures

8. Testing Results

9. Evaluations

10. Professional Development

All of the information you will use to teach your lessons should be very accessible. Some folders can even include materials for subjects you'd like to teach in the future, and you can add to these files as you come across additional ideas. Folders on various units or themes are a helpful way to keep lessons together so they can be pulled out at a moment's notice. In addition, you may want to establish a drawer in the file cabinet for each subject area or course that you teach. Once again, this system is entirely yours to develop, but you must start a system for storing vital information soon. When the pupils enter your classroom, you'll be too preoccupied to even think about filing anything for quite a while!

Updating Your Files

Don't forget to weed through and update these files periodically. After you finish your first year of teaching, you should look through the stuff that you've accumulated to see what you actually utilized. If you come across something that you never even touched, you should probably consider getting rid of it—or perhaps move it to the "think about trashing" part of your filing system. Many teachers go though their materials at the end of every school year, while others feel that it's better to clean and tidy things up before school begins. The choice about when to do "spring cleaning" is up to you—just don't forget to do it!

PERSONAL TIME

All teachers balance tight schedules. In addition to their classes, there are early-morning and after-school meetings, parent phone calls, conferences, photocopying, and planning time to fit into a single day. If you don't keep track of all that you need to do for your new job, you may discover that you don't have one next year. Your organizational skills will certainly be something that your evaluator will be watching during this initial year on the job.

As I mentioned earlier, learning to keep a calendar for the curriculum is a key component of becoming a competent teacher. This is also true of your own personal time and commitments. If you don't have a plan book, be sure to get one from the secretary or person in charge of supplies. As you fill this out week by week, be sure to note exactly when and where you need to be for meetings and special assignments. (There will be more information on the plan book in Chapter 4.)

In addition, you should record important dates on your own personal calendar (also called a daily planner). If you don't own a daily planner, go to a local office supply or stationery store and find one that would work for you. Start by jotting down the date that teachers report back to school. Circle or highlight the first day of school! Write down any meetings that you already know about as well as calendared events like Back-to-School Night or Parent Conferences. Be sure that you keep your personal calendar/daily planner with you at all times and compare it to your teacher plan book at least once a week to confirm that all dates match up.

As an educator, you will have many things to keep track of in this busy profession. The plan book for teaching and your own personal calendar/daily planner will be the literal center for your teaching experience. Your daily planner will allow you to keep important dates clearly marked—and you can use it to make sure you actually maintain some type of personal life as well! The plan book will store the specific tasks you will be doing with your students, as well as any vital school information.

No matter what your personal style of organization has been up to this point, you have the opportunity to make some changes at this exciting juncture in your life and career. Take advantage of the time before school starts to study ways of cataloging the curriculum as well as the contents of your classroom. But don't try to tackle it all in one day! Focus on one area, like your files or storage cabinet, and don't move on to anything else until you've got it mastered. Once you've arranged your materials and figured out how you're going to manage the requirements of the upcoming school year, you'll be ready to meet your new students with a smile.

Tips to Remember

1. If you need more help with organizational skills, pick up a book that can guide you down the road to success (see Resource B, Recommended Reading, for selections by Jenson or Covey). There are numerous sources that can give you specific ideas on how to get your professional and personal life in better shape!

2. Be sure to ask other teachers who work at your same grade level or in your subject area how they plan to cover the curriculum. Many of them will be glad to sit down with you and give you specific suggestions.

3. Make a "wish list" of items that the school can't provide for you right now. Share this with parents, community members, church groups, and service organizations that can help out. Many people want to assist teachers and students, but they must have an idea of what is needed.

4

Planning the Trip

Your Plan Book Can Be Your Best Friend

Order is contagious; so is disorder.

—Author unknown

"They're sending all of us to auctioneering class.
If we learn to talk faster, we'll be able to get through
the whole textbook by the end of the year."

Like a hiker preparing to head out on his or her next adventure, you've been busy gathering the supplies and equipment you'll need to set out on your amazing journey into education. You have also spent time thinking about your classroom structure and how best to prepare for the diverse learners you'll be working with very soon. Now you're ready to complete the final stage of this preparation process before the school year begins: planning the actual path that you and your students will take.

Although most excursions involve following established roads, the trek into teaching allows you to blaze your own trail. You'll need to follow some basic guidelines regarding the curriculum, but you'll soon find there's an enormous amount of freedom to choose how and where you want your students to travel. In the beginning, this liberty can be a bit disconcerting—that's why the plan book will become one of your very best friends!

During my years of teaching, I found that advanced preparation kept me and my students on course. Sometimes it can be the stabilizing force in an otherwise crazy day. I'm sure you've experienced the benefit of having a daily calendar or schedule to guide you so that, even when unexpected events unfold, you can simply refer back to your original plans to get things back on track.

In school settings, many interruptions can occur without any advanced warning. For example, one day I had an experiment planned for three different science classes, but an unexpected assembly (a Major League baseball player was able to fit our school into his schedule) changed things. Two groups missed the science lab, but I was able to move another activity and finish this activity with them on the following day. Because I had the week already outlined in the plan book, I didn't have to stress about this momentary glitch in the curriculum. Sometimes we had emergency drills (they're not always announced to the faculty) or the computers in the lab weren't working, so I had to restructure the day. Having lessons outlined in the plan book allowed me to adjust to these impromptu events with relative ease.

There are as many shapes, sizes, and varieties of educational plan books as there are personal organizers. Some schools will automatically offer one to you—or you can ask for the "standard issue" that they have in stock. If they don't provide this helpful tool, or if you aren't satisfied with that particular style, go to a local teacher supply store to see what's available. You may be able to locate the perfect model in a catalog or online. Your main focus should be to find a product that pleases you and will allow you to get organized for your new class.

More than likely, you became familiar with using a plan book during your student teaching experience. As you may recall, each page should have large, open blocks that will enable you to clearly write your daily plans for each class that you teach. You can decide how you want this tool to work for you, but taking a look at other teachers' methods may be useful as well. Be sure to label your plan book with your name, school, room number, and school telephone number in permanent ink. By doing so, should it become lost (heaven help you!), someone will know where to return it. I recommend that you keep your plan book close to you—like you would your wallet or keys. It truly will become a cornerstone of your professional life.

DAY-BY-DAY PLANNING

Prepare in Advance

Did you ever work with teachers who scribbled a few lines or notes to themselves right before the morning bell rang? Unfortunately, these short blurbs of information actually became their lessons plans for the day! I don't recommend this system for anyone in education, unless you need to make last-minute changes or some emergency has occurred. Even the most experienced educators should prepare in advance so that they can meet the demands of modern classrooms. *A sign of a true professional is the advanced care and planning that goes into that person's career* (Wong & Wong, 1998). Think about how you would feel if you walked into a doctor's office only to find that your chart wasn't there, the receptionist had lost track of what time everyone was scheduled for appointments, and the nurse scurried about trying to clean and organize items for your visit. You'd probably want to get out of there as fast as your feet could carry you!

Sadly, this is the scenario in some classrooms—but the students can't escape from the educational malpractice! There are a few teachers who feel that they can simply "wing it" once they get the curriculum down, but they merely appear flighty and flaky to any observant eye. Today's students are quite savvy, and they realize when a teacher doesn't have a structured class. In these disorganized settings, chaos is likely to erupt. Unprepared teachers usually experience discipline problems and struggle with completing the required curriculum. Strategic methods for organizing the class structure and content flow must be established from the first day of school and consistently maintained as the year continues (Weinstein, 1996; Wong & Wong, 1998).

Prepare to Be Flexible

One of the best and simplest recommendations I can give you is to be sure to use a pencil when planning. Why? Mostly because you'll be doing a lot of erasing and changing as the days go by. Yes, even in education the best of plans oft go awry! You could have beautiful, detailed notes on all that you want to accomplish, but an unannounced fire drill can throw you off by twenty minutes. You'll need to continue that fabulous lesson on the following day. As I've mentioned, an unexpected assembly or guest speaker can completely rearrange your agenda, or your students might require more review time than you expected before the exam. Or you might find that simply switching one lesson for another makes more sense once you've started a new unit. The ability to neatly maneuver items in your itinerary will help you feel more organized.

Don't Forget the Homework

As I mentioned, the plan book will allow you to write down short descriptions of what you want to accomplish on a given day as well as throughout that week. You will also be able to jot down ideas for the weeks and months ahead. As the school year progresses, you will be able to reflect back on the lessons that you've already covered to be certain that you hit particular topics. Most important, don't forget to write down the homework that will be assigned for each class period. This will enable you to clearly see what should be collected or corrected at the beginning of the next lesson. Box 4.1 includes some helpful items that you should include in your professional plan book.

As the knowledge base continues to expand at exponential rates, there are more and more requirements for teachers to fulfill. This alone should make written plans a necessity for all of your professional experiences. Many districts impose various

Box 4.1

PLAN BOOK CONTENT CHECKLIST

- ☐ Label the cover with your name in dark ink.

- ☐ Print your school's name and phone number, as well as your room number, on the first inside page.

- ☐ Try to use a "week at a glance" format, with blocks for each day and class.

- ☐ Use an extra column to keep track of all school meetings (don't forget to include the time and place).

- ☐ Block out any special events (assemblies, pep rallies, guest speakers, testing).

- ☐ Highlight reminders like important phone calls that must be made on specific days.

- ☐ Post all homework assigned in your plan book so there is never a question about what is due the next day, week, or month.

- ☐ Include dates to remember, like local, state, national, and global celebrations.

- ☐ Add personal, schoolwide, and district goals in an extra column from time to time as reminders of what you are striving toward during this school year.

requirements for new employees; be sure to check out these procedures with your principal if this isn't discussed at the new teacher orientation meeting. Typically, written lessons must be available any time one of your supervisors or administrators pays a visit.

The plan book will assist you in organizing daily lessons in a concise, clear manner. As you look at what needs to be accomplished during each day, week, and month of the school year, you'll feel more comfortable and confident about the structure of your class. Your students will also have the chance to receive the optimum educational experience that you can offer because of your forethought.

KEEPING YOUR CLASS RUNNING SMOOTHLY

As I explain to my preservice teachers, once you've been hired into a position, the administrators will automatically assume that you know your subject matter (or else your college or university wouldn't have allowed you to graduate). Their primary concern, particularly during the first school year, will be whether or not you can manage a classroom. A major factor in maintaining discipline and control is thorough planning and preparation throughout your day. When you have every minute organized, the students typically will stay on task because there won't be any opportunity *not* to do so. Even "free time" should be scheduled into your lesson. (More information on classroom management will be covered in Chapter 6.)

Time on Task

There has been increased emphasis in schools concerning "time on task," partially because of studies that have revealed how much time can be wasted during the course of the school day (Weinstein, 1996). Even small jobs such as taking roll, reading announcements, and collecting or passing out papers devour precious minutes that we have to work with our students. As you start to structure your lesson plans, think about ways to avoid this professional pitfall. Always include an opening activity, such as a "quick write" on a topic you'll be discussing. How about turning on the overhead so that students can work on a math problem or two that will review yesterday's lesson? Once you train students that you'll be expecting them to start some meaningful task as soon as they enter your class, it will become a habit for them. While they are working, you can quickly take roll; then you can move on to the awesome lesson you have outlined in your plan book.

"Bell Ringer"

Substitute Lessons

Another terrific asset of a teacher plan book is that it can be utilized to create substitute lessons should you get sick. Some teachers will leave their plan books open on their desks at the end of the school day in case of an emergency. Other educators simply can't leave the campus without this vital tool packed safely away in a briefcase or tote bag. With the accessibility of fax machines at most schools, it is easy to send lesson plans to the school office, or you can call the school secretary and explain what the substitute should do. Quite possibly, your site will require that you prepare a specific packet for substitutes; be sure to check on these procedures. No matter what happens, you will soon discover that advanced preparation will make your life easier, and you'll be able to relax if a problem does arise, knowing that your class will run smoothly without you.

PUTTING IT ALL TOGETHER

If you are an organizer by nature, then setting up a plan book will be a snap. If, however, you are more relaxed in style, I can only encourage you to take the initiative to implement these ideas during the early weeks of your new job. Like many areas in life, we *can* change old patterns if we put forth some effort and energy, and I can guarantee that the time you invest in using a plan book will pay off in numerous ways throughout your career. Not only will you appear more professional, but your students also will benefit from your exceptionally well-prepared lessons!

With all of the information that you must organize during this first year of teaching, it is important that you keep track of everything in a user-friendly format. From the start of the new year to the last day of school, you should have a written plan for each and every class you'll teach. Write down a short outline or key ideas that you wish to accomplish, as well as any *fillers* you could implement should your lesson run a little short. Keep a stack of word searches, crossword puzzles, or short readings with questions handy for "free-time" activities.

By the way, don't try to plan too far in advance! I suggest working out detailed lessons no more than two weeks ahead, although you certainly can make notations of chapters, key concepts, or projects that you want to accomplish by certain dates (refer to your calendar that we discussed in Chapter 3). Your principal might schedule a major school event, or perhaps an unexpected teacher inservice day will interrupt your plans. It can be frustrating to have to redo weeks of work, so plan cautiously. Also, why not sit down on Thursday or Friday afternoon and begin organizing the lessons for the upcoming week? This way you can gather the supplies for your lesson, get copies made, and make a list of anything you will need to pull together before the next week arrives.

There are numerous strategies for successful planning, and you will need to experiment until you find what works best with your teaching style (Jensen & Kiley, 2000). When you opt for more structure in your life, you will soon feel more like a professional! You'll also gain the confidence that you can create a consistent, controlled environment where optimum learning will take place. As with any journey in life, success doesn't happen by accident. Your adventure will take a lot of advanced thought and preparation. And, although you'll have a few unexpected events from time to time, you'll enjoy the process of designing the perfect educational experience for your students.

Tips to Remember

1. If you aren't satisfied with commercial plan books, create one of your own. Use blank paper, markers, and a three-ring binder to develop one that you'll feel comfortable using.

2. The plan book is also a good place to post other important information that you may need on a regular basis. The bell schedule, school map, vital phone numbers, and even seating charts can become part of this indispensable tool.

3. Keep your plan book in the same place each day to avoid having to scramble to find it once the class begins. There's no point in having beautifully prepared lessons if you can't get to them promptly.

4. Check with your principal about the school's policy concerning substitute plans. You may be required to put together an emergency plan packet to leave in the office "just in case." Always keep at least one set of "any day" plans on your desk so that someone could take over your class in a pinch!

5

ENTER THE STUDENTS!

Meeting the Demands of Diverse Learners

The human heart has hidden treasures, in secret kept, in silence sealed.

—Charlotte Brontë, *Evening Solace*

"So what if I didn't get the same answer as you. Doesn't our school encourage diversity?"

The day that you've been working, planning, and waiting for has finally arrived! Soon your new students will be at the classroom door, as eager as you are to discover what awaits them this school year. Whether they are five-year-olds or nearing eighteen, all kids worry about what their teacher will be like and how he or she will respond to them. Everything from your initial greeting to your tone of voice and facial expressions can greatly affect the *first impressions* that the students have about you.

The good news is that you've spent enough time around young people to have an idea of what makes them tick! Remember, each child is an individual with specific needs and desires. To impact the lives of these learners, teachers must understand the unique qualities that comprise the human mind, spirit, and soul. All of the students you come in contact with are special, and it is your privilege and responsibility to discover what makes each one so extraordinary. Becoming an expert on the young people who will be in your care during this school year should be one of your primary goals during the first few weeks of school.

"WHO AM I?" MEETING YOUR STUDENTS

When the students enter your classroom, they bring with them a wealth of knowledge, experiences, and abilities. They are not a "blank slate," as an old theory of learning once espoused, but rather a treasure chest awaiting the right key to open up the vast resources inside. Sometimes a simple smile and friendly welcome that first day of school will do the trick, but for other kids, you will have to look long and hard for the magical means to uncover the mysteries lying deep within them.

As you call off each name during attendance, pay careful attention to pronunciation. Let them say it to you if you struggle, and be sure to apologize for any errors. Phonetically write out how the names sound, and practice these until you get them right (I used to tell my students that I tended to be a slow learner when it came to names, so I hoped they'd be patient with me!). Be sure to ask if they would rather be called by a nickname—many middle- and high-school students do. *Remember, names are an essential part of "who we are," so it's important to start learning them from the very first day.*

As you get to know your students, you will quickly notice their individual characteristics and personalities. Obviously, there are the gender differences. We could spend several chapters describing in detail how the X- and Y-chromosomes create so many wonderfully distinct differences! You'll observe that some kids are tall while others are short. Many children wear glasses or even contacts. Some of your students will be dressed in the hottest fashions, while others may have only one or two nice outfits for school.

Culturally Diverse Learners

Because of our nation's history of cultural diversity as well as continuing demographic changes, you might notice that your class is ethnically diverse. In some cases, this diversity may not be as visually evident, but the cultural roots of each child will be unique. Be aware of these differences as you interact with your class, as well as how students' experiences may differ from your own background, heritage, perspectives, and learning style. You will want to offer opportunities for your students to share about their culture and experiences. *Try to envision how the rich diversity of your students will enhance your curriculum and instruction this year!*

Culturally Proficient Teaching

Many experts in the field of education will tell you that the demographics of our student population are changing at a rapid rate (Banks, 1994; Nieto, 2000). The number of "minority" groups in schools has increased dramatically so that, in many areas, they are the "majority." Unfortunately, many of the instructional methods employed in schools during the 20th century simply were unsuccessful in meeting the needs of our ethnically diverse children (Darling-Hammond, 1997). Part of the problem was that we expected everyone to assimilate, to take on the attributes of an "American" lifestyle, while leaving behind whatever past experiences and characteristics of culture these new members of society brought to the table (Spring, 1998). We have seen tremendous progress in the broadening of our definition of what it means to be a member of the American culture during the past few decades, especially in the inclusion of language, culture, and ethnicity as an important part of what makes this nation great (Banks, 1994; Nieto, 2000; Spring, 1998).

As diversity increased in our communities and schools during the second half of the 20th century, it became painfully apparent that our educational institutions were failing to link ethnically and linguistically diverse students to academic success, as evidenced by poor academic performance and high dropout rates (Darling-Hammond, 1997). As some researchers and educators suggest, the primary problem was that we were not able to make a connection with "who" the students were as individuals (Banks, 1994).

Linguistic Diversity

I mention *linguistically* diverse because language plays such a tremendous role in the acquisition of knowledge. With the ability to speak, write, and read comes access to the world around us, but many students, especially those who are new to this country, have yet to receive this key to success. As an educator, you must know your students' level of English language ability. Many educators will have ESL (English as a Second Language) students mainstreamed into their classes. Perhaps you have decided that you'd like to teach those who need help gaining access to English. If you need an introduction to issues of language learning, I recommend that you read *The Natural Approach* by Krashen and Terrell for a basic understanding of the principles of language acquisition (see Resource B, Recommended Reading).

Inclusive Curriculum and Instruction

In response to many of the inadequacies in our methodologies, some teachers have begun to implement a *multicultural* curriculum as well as utilize techniques that will tap into the experiences and backgrounds of all children, thus helping to open the doors to their academic success (Noel, 2000; Sleeter & Grant, 2000). There is growing evidence that inclusion of topics related to culture and diversity within mainstream classrooms positively impacts attitudes of prejudice and stereotyping in students (Wilke, 1997).

The inclusion of multicultural concepts is relatively easy for an educator who is dedicated to making the curriculum more meaningful to students. It involves the infusing of a wide variety of materials that bring cultural topics and discussions into everyday activities and lessons. As a new teacher, you can begin by studying the curriculum, textbooks, and supplementary materials that you will be using with your students. Do they reflect the rich array of ethnicity and diversity that comprise your class? If not, you may need to look for activities, posters, music, books, and so forth that will help all of the children in your class feel that they are a part of the learning process.

Clearly, this is a timely topic for teachers in today's classrooms. Look for a book on culture, language, and/or diversity issues to read in your spare time. Educators can always learn more about these concerns as we continue on our journey to becoming more culturally competent. By reading up on this topic, you will glean ideas on how to encourage your students to become more accepting of diversity in the world in which they live. Part of the key to a successful school year is acquiring an understanding of *who* your students are as individuals. Once you've connected with them at that level, they'll be ready to learn anything! Some educators describe this as creating an "inviting" versus "uninviting" classroom. When students feel accepted, appreciated, and, yes, invited into the learning process, you greatly increase the probability of student learning (Wong & Wong, 1998).

THE MIND MATTERS

Normally it is the process of teaching and learning that takes center stage in any educational environment, but, as we've learned, it is essential that educators understand their students at a much deeper level than simply names on the class roster before attempting to teach them anything. *This process involves getting to know what makes each one of your students tick, what kinds of things they like to learn, and what previous knowledge they bring to the table.*

Assess Ability Levels and Prior Knowledge

In addition to interacting with them on a one-on-one basis, you might also start by surveying the class to see what they've done in your subject area before. Many teachers either create or use a standardized assessment tool to determine the various levels and abilities of their students. Something as simple as having the students write a short paragraph (for younger kids) or one-page essay (middle- or highschoolers) to adequately assess their knowledge on a topic can be extremely helpful to formulate a clear picture of what these learners already know.

Review Diagnostic Data

In addition, you may want to review diagnostic data that is available for each of your students. This may be readily accessible (some schools will provide you with copies of these types of records when you receive your class list), or you may have to investigate on your own by looking into their cumulative files. Some teachers prefer to begin the school year without any preconceived notions about the students, believing that this allows the students the freedom to start out fresh. No matter how much investigation you choose to do, realize that it takes some time to truly understand your students' abilities as well as their learning styles.

Assess Learning Styles

As you know from your own experiences in education, each of us acquires information differently, and sometimes the instructor's methods are incompatible with these learning pathways. Think back to when you were a student. Which teachers did you connect with and why? Were there teaching styles that simply clashed with how you learned best? Reflecting upon these situations will help you analyze your own methods of learning and perhaps give you insights about how you can improve your presentation techniques. For example, highly visual learners can easily become frustrated by a teacher who gives all instruction orally to the class. There are hands-on learners—the kind who take apart the VCR and put it back together again without the instruction book—who struggle when they are asked to write and read all day. Your students will acquire information in a variety of ways. Be sure that your instructional methods address all of their needs.

Getting a better grasp on how the mind works is not easy, even for brain researchers! As we strive toward excellence for our students, it is critical that we make a concerted effort to understand these concepts. As a new teacher, one of your first tasks will be to learn about the ability levels of *all* your students. Make time now to read books on brain-based learning, constructivist theory, active learning, and multicultural education. Attend workshops and in-services that will increase your knowledge about optimum ways to help your students become more successful in academic settings as well as in whatever the future holds for them.

SPECIAL NEEDS

As this exciting adventure into teaching unfolds, you will immediately discover that there are a variety of students with special needs within your classroom. Sometimes you will have kids who have been identified as "special ed." These students will have a special education class that they attend for part or most of the day, and they are simply being mainstreamed into your class in order to experience as much normalcy in their educational experience as possible. *This process, called inclusion, has numerous benefits for everyone involved in the educational process* (Smith, Polloway, Patton, & Dowdy, 1998).

Depending upon their needs and abilities, those in special education may have an aide with them the entire time or for part of the day. Your job as the teacher is to make these students feel welcome and part of the class community while at the same time providing educational instruction at their ability levels (Shea & Bauer, 1997). Part of the delicate balance of teaching that you must begin to practice is meeting these special needs while at the same time keeping all of your other students on track with the curriculum. This isn't an easy task, so asking for ideas from fellow teachers— especially the special education teachers—will be essential.

Individualized Education Plans (IEPs)

To better comprehend the needs of children in special education, you will probably be included in the Individualized Education Plan (IEP) process as well as other meetings held by the special education teachers. It is imperative that you attend these meetings so that you can fully understand what you can do to assist your students. In addition, these specialized teachers and aides will often fill you in on any important details that you should be aware of while planning your lessons. Some of them may have worked with these students for years and will have terrific insights into their learning styles. They would be happy to schedule appointments with you, but informal discussions in the halls or at lunch will help answer some of the questions that may arise as you interact with certain students. You should also research the students' cumulative files to see what diagnostic information is available.

Learning Disabilities

There will also be Learning Disabled (LD) students in many classrooms. Learning disabilities are described as discrepancies between ability and achievement; for example, a student may be performing below grade level in an area like reading or writing (Shea & Bauer, 1997). Once again, you should attend all meetings with the specialists, psychologists, and parents who are invested in the lives of these children and can assist you in developing lessons that will increase their opportunities for success. Physical handicaps are usually apparent, but some teachers are unaware of how much students with these disabilities can actually do. In particular, physical education teachers must know the strengths and weaknesses of the students with physical disabilities so they can include students in as many activities as possible (Shea & Bauer, 1997; Smith et al., 1998).

Attention-Deficit/Hyperactivity Disorder (ADHD)

There has also been an increase in the number of students identified with Attention-Deficit/Hyperactivity Disorder (ADHD). Experts describe ADHD as "brain differences" that are exhibited by impulsiveness, lack of focus, difficulty following multiple-step instructions, and hyperactive behavior (Wehman, 1997). As a classroom teacher, you must be cognizant of any students who may have this disability. There are specific steps that you can take to help ensure their success at school. In addition, their parents and doctors may want you to assist in evaluating how their medication is working during the hours that they are in your class. Some of your students may need to take medicine for diabetes, heart conditions, or other problems, so you will want to keep an eye on their status while they are with you. You will be notified about this by school officials (for example, the school nurse or an administrator), and often the parents themselves will want to meet with you before the school year begins to discuss their concerns. You can learn more about the specific requirements for caring for these students from the school nurse, psychologist, special education personnel, and parents (Shea & Bauer, 1997).

All Students Are Special

Although there will be many children in your classes who will require special attention, the main point to take away from this chapter is that all children are special. *Each student that enters your room is carrying an invisible backpack full of experiences, interesting data, language, strengths, weaknesses, cultural nuances, heritage, needs, and desires!* As the children look at you with those wide, inquisitive eyes, realize that there's a vast wealth of knowledge and experiences lying deep within them. Like you, each one is a fascinating human being, full of life and a zest for learning, and he or she is eagerly anticipating the school year that's about to unfold. Take stock of all of this, then open the door to your heart, soul, and mind—and let the learning begin!

Tips to Remember

1. Do some type of "Who Am I?" activity that first day of school. Students can write essays, draw pictures, fill in a fun form—anything that will let them begin telling you more about themselves will be invaluable! Also, why not share your own "Who Am I?" with your students?

2. Look over your curriculum and materials for the school year. Do they include all of the diversity that's represented by your students? If not, immediately begin looking for ways that you can include their culture, language, ethnicity, and so forth, in your teaching and classroom environment.

3. Attend cultural events in the community so that you can become more familiar with the heritage of the students and parents that you'll be working with during the school year.

4. Talk to your fellow teachers about student concerns. Many of them will have awesome suggestions on how to improve your teaching techniques—more than you'll find in a whole collection of books on education!

6

The First Month of the Journey

The child mind is a citadel that can be taken neither by stealth nor by storm; but there is a natural way of approach and a gate of easy entry always open to him who knows how to find it.

—Author unknown

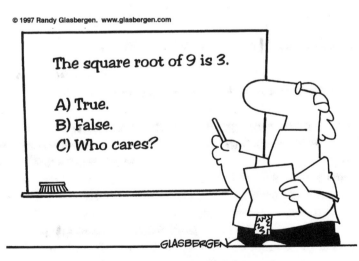

Many students actually look forward to Mr. Atwadder's math tests.

Every year, daring adventurers try to climb one of the most treacherous mountains on earth. Everest looms high in the Himalayas, luring young and old alike to test their skills on its slippery slopes and ever-changing landscape. You may have seen television footage of teams who have attempted this arduous ascent. Some have been successful, while others have returned in defeat. What qualities or skills have the small percentage of people possessed who plunged a flag into that final mountain peak? In part, their success was due to advance preparation and in-depth research of the right routes to take. For certain victors, their strength of spirit and a commitment to complete the task at hand fortified them against some of the fiercest forces of nature.

Fortunately, you won't have to wear protective gear or take along oxygen tanks for your trek into teaching, but you'll definitely have some hills to climb and rough roads to cover. You're heading out on a trail that you've never been down before, and there will be obstacles around certain corners that will test all of your skills and abilities. With the first day of school quickly approaching, it is time to review your plans and be certain that you are as prepared as you possibly can be for the events that lie ahead of you.

THE "WHEN," THE "WHERE," AND THE "WHO"

The Days Before the First Day of Class

Whenever I take a vacation, there are always a few last-minute details that need my attention. This is certainly true for teachers as they get ready for the exciting first day of school! In fact, that is why most districts require that teachers and other staff members report for duty several days to a week before classes begin. During those preparation days, your principal will have meetings scheduled with faculty members to be sure that the whole team is focused and ready to receive the students. He or she will also go over any new goals or curriculum. More than likely, you will have grade level or department meetings so that the teachers in these areas can discuss any items of concern, as well as be sure that they are "on the same page" when it comes to teaching strategies, new standards, testing mandates, and innovative programs that must be implemented.

As a new person on campus, you will want to get a good working knowledge of the "physical plant," or work site. This will assist you in feeling more comfortable with your surroundings, and that confidence will be obvious to your students. Be sure that you are familiar with all of the buildings and facilities on your campus. Get a map from the school secretary and walk around the buildings several times before classes begin. You should know the following locations so that you can give students quick directions if needed:

KEY LOCATIONS FOR YOUR SCHOOL MAP

- Main office
- Nurse's office
- Bathrooms, for students and for faculty
- Cafeteria
- Gymnasium
- Library
- Physical education fields
- Telephones (again, for students as well as staff)
- Counseling and/or psychologist's office
- Special education rooms
- Copy center
- Custodial workroom
- Faculty work areas

Meet Your Colleagues in the Building

Principals usually help orient new staff to the campus, especially so they will know what to do in case of an emergency. If you have questions about your school's crisis plans, be sure to ask someone in the office to explain procedures to you. While touring the campus, stop into the classrooms that have the door open and introduce yourself to some of your colleagues. This will help other staff members get to know you, and you'll be able to start placing names and faces together. I would especially recommend that you do this with anyone that you'll be working with directly—for example, other members of your department, the resource or special education teachers, bilingual or ESL (English as a Second Language) specialists, and the custodian. (In Chapter 8 you will find other information about key people you should become familiar with on your new campus.)

Learn About Your New Community

If you are new to the community where your school is located, it would be beneficial to take a drive around the area before the first day of school. Get to know the neighborhoods, shopping malls, parks, and hangouts of your new environment. This way, you'll begin absorbing some of the culture of your school. Familiarize yourself with the schools that are nearby. You may even want to use some of the services that various businesses in the area offer. For example, the local bookstore will be a great resource for materials that you may use in your class. One food market near a school where I worked served specialty foods for the ethnic groups in our area. I was able to try different types of cuisine that my students enjoyed at home. Also, you will get to know community members as well as parents as you interact in their environment.

By all means, keep your ears open for special community events so you can get more involved. In one small town where I taught, they held an annual rodeo. I put my boots on and joined in the fun. Not only did I soak up the local culture, but I also got to see some of my students participate in this interesting event. Keeping connected with the community is an important part of success within our classrooms and schools (Darling-Hammond, 1997).

THE "HOW" AND THE "WHAT"

Although you've spent a great deal of time perusing the content you'll be teaching during the school year as well as developing interesting, engaging lessons, you can never invest enough time studying the strategies and techniques you plan to implement in your classes. Imagine if a rock climber had to wonder, while clinging to the sheer face of a mountain, if she'd brought along enough rope. That won't happen if she was willing to spend a few extra minutes checking her gear before she ever left home. This is the same type of final review that you should make before you actually get the school year started. Taking time to assess your curriculum and teaching methodology one last time is never wasteful! While you're making your final assessment, the two most important things to think about are the "how" and the "what" of teaching.

Instructional Techniques

The "how" of education is a simple description of the instructional techniques that you plan to use with your students. In other words, what specific methods do you intend to implement that will help them learn? For example, when you thought about whether you wanted students in rows or at tables, part of this decision was made based upon how you are going to interact with the students (and how they are going to interact with one another). Perhaps you selected a U-shaped design. Maybe you want the tables or desks grouped together for cooperative learning (Johnson, Johnson, & Holubec, 1994). Take one last look at your classroom to make certain that it is arranged appropriately for the style of teaching that you will implement most.

As you review your lesson plan for the first week of school, have you considered all of the instructional methods that you plan to use? Will there be individual or quiet work times? If so, have you noted this in your plan book? As you give the students opportunities to share and learn in larger group settings, have you considered the behavioral expectations you'll need to explain to the students before such activities begin? (Additional ideas on some basic concepts of classroom management will be discussed later in this chapter.)

Curriculum and Content

The "what" of education is the curriculum that you will be covering throughout the school year. Perhaps you've had adequate time to review everything you've been asked to teach, but this is not always the case for many teachers. Because of budget limitations and other constraints, some educators are not hired until right before school begins. In extreme circumstances, like a sudden increase in student population, the school may even be filling new positions during the first few weeks of class! Also, grade level and course assignments can be changed to reflect enrollment—even at the last minute. Whatever time you have during these initial days of preparation, be sure to carefully study the textbooks, curriculum guides, and supplementary materials that are available for your class. This will not only help you feel more adequately prepared to teach your students, but you will also be able to answer that one inevitable question: *"What will we be studying this year?"*

New Teacher Support and Mentoring

Many school districts now provide assistance for first- and even second-year teachers. In some parts of the country, this help is mandatory. The people selected for this task are experienced teachers who serve as "mentors" for newer faculty members. They could be professionals from your school site, or they may travel around to numerous schools assisting other educators. Before the school year begins, find out who these mentors are and whether one will be automatically assigned to you. If your district does not offer these services, then try to network with another teacher in your department or grade level who will be able to answer questions or give advice as the year goes along. As you work on getting a handle on the curriculum and various teaching techniques, don't be afraid to seek guidance from others who were in your same place in this educational journey not that long ago.

INTRODUCING YOUR KIDS!

That first day of school has finally arrived! It will be full of excitement, angst, and a certain amount of the unexpected. If you've got that strange sensation of butterflies circling in your stomach, you're not alone. After almost two decades of teaching, I still feel them fluttering. *These feelings help all of us remember the emotions that our students are also experiencing as they enter our classrooms!* As they take their seats and stare at you with inquisitive eyes, realize that they are breathlessly waiting to see if you are all that they hoped and prayed you'd be, too!

Years ago, when I had just begun my career in education, I heard Jerry Lewis use a wonderful expression on his annual Muscular Dystrophy Association Telethon. He called the MDA children "his kids." Any stigma that had been attached to those suffering from muscular dystrophy seemed to wash away before the public's eyes with the new label of "Jerry's kids." I decided that this was how I was going to approach my students—they would be like my own children during the hours that they were with me at school. Like a parent, I would protect, provide and care for, and look out for their best interests.

You're an Important Adult in Their Lives

One day I referred to the students in my class as "my kids." A young man in the back of the classroom quickly retorted, "We're not your kids, Mrs. Wilke." I stopped and looked at him for a minute. Did he think that I was trying to replace his parents? I couldn't tell from his expression, so I simply shared what was in my heart. "Well, I like to think of you as my kids during the day. Then I feel like we're one big happy family." He stared at me for a few seconds; suddenly the biggest grin that I had seen all year appeared on his face. I think he liked that idea, too.

How might this kind of perspective impact your teaching? The 30 or so young hearts and minds that will be entering your classroom are yours for the busiest, most profitable hours of their day. Some educators may also see 30-something students the second hour of the day, then more the third hour, and on and on as the day goes along. In other words, many middle- and high-school teachers will have a hundred or more students to take care of before three o'clock rolls around! Whatever the numbers, you will play an essential part in each of their lives—academically, emotionally, socially, and psychologically. You may touch a life that never receives a word of encouragement outside of your classroom walls. Although some of your students may be in your class for only a month or two before their family moves or they're transferred elsewhere, they'll know within a few days whether or not you truly care about them.

Teacher Appreciation Day Can Last a Lifetime

Many years ago while working at a small K-8 school, a group of parents asked the students to write notes to their instructors for Teacher Appreciation Day. I will never forget two of the cards I received. One boy, who was new to the country and could barely write English, penned a short message that said he wished that he could be in my class forever! Another was from a shy young lady who rarely said a word in class. Her letter, signed with her name and a huge red heart, expressed that I was the best teacher she ever had because I smiled at her each morning! I still look at these notes from time to time, especially on those days when I wonder if I'm making a difference in this world!

As you begin to focus on your new students, realize that you have the potential to impact their lives in immeasurable ways. You might be the one educator who makes a student realize that he or she can go to college. Maybe you'll be the positive influence that keeps certain kids away from gangs and drugs. Perhaps you'll be the only person who gives a young man or woman a reason to get up each morning and go on with life. And wouldn't it be wonderful to be your students' favorite teacher—the one that they will tell their own kids about someday?

INTRODUCING THEIR TEACHER!

You're in the Spotlight

The first day of school provides you with the perfect opportunity to take center stage for a few hours. If being in a drama or headlining at the local theater was not part of your life's ambition, it's too late! You're in the spotlight as soon as those students enter your room. They will want to know everything that they can about you (of course, you don't want to give all of your secrets away the first day), and the tone that you set during those initial hours will be essential to the classroom environment that you want to establish. This is your chance to acquaint the students with your expectations and the requirements that they will be asked to fulfill (Weinstein, 1996; Wong & Wong, 1998). *You should let them know you're human while at the same time exuding that professional persona that is vital for respect in the classroom.*

Handouts

It would be helpful to have handouts to give the students as you explain your courses. A simple syllabus is recommended at the middle-school and high-school levels. Upper elementary to high-school students should have copies of your classroom discipline procedures (more on this later). Important phone numbers and e-mail addresses should be given out on the first day so that students and parents can contact you or the school when they have questions or concerns. There may be a homework hotline or even a school web site that you want the students to have. Be sure to prepare these handouts in advance so you can send them home that first day.

They Want to Please You

Remember, most of the students are hoping to learn all that they can about you so that they can meet your expectations. Most children are "people-pleasers" by nature; many only need to know what you want in order to begin working away. Of course, you will have some students who are going to test you for a few weeks to see if you truly merit their respect and cooperation. Keep cool, smile, but hold firm to your convictions so they will quickly discover that you mean business.

BEHAVIORAL EXPECTATIONS

Many experienced teachers will tell you that your success or failure during the school year will depend upon two things:

1. The *expectations and rules* that you establish on the first day of school

2. How you follow through with the *consequences* that you've established

You may have thought I was going to say something about what you are supposed to teach this year, great lesson planning, or exciting activities. Believe it or not, those things are simply not as vital as establishing good ground rules for how students are expected to act in your classroom. Once you have a well-controlled, disciplined class, learning will naturally take place. I've seen all types of teachers over the years, and the ones who operated by the seat of their pants or chose to let things slide in their classroom suffered all year long. Unfortunately, so did their students.

Classroom Management

Behavioral control within the learning environment is better known as "classroom management" (Weinstein, 1996). As I mentioned, many children are innately well behaved and want to please their teachers no matter what, but other kids are not blessed with such easygoing, compliant natures. There are some young people with strong personalities who would much rather run the show themselves than have you try to teach anything. It is imperative, therefore, that you let all the students know from the beginning who is in charge of your classroom (Curwin & Mendler, 1999).

This is not to say that you shouldn't let students feel that they are a part of the learning process. Yet, even if you believe in the "teacher as facilitator" model of education, it is still your duty to act as the guide and gauge for all classroom behaviors and activities. If you fail to do so, not only could chaos erupt, but you might also be jobless after your first year of experience. *Many administrators are looking for teachers who can manage classrooms effectively, because they know that good learning can only take place when order and discipline are the rule rather than the exception.*

Classroom Rules

Once you've introduced yourself and gone over the essential components of the course, clearly explain your classroom rules. It is a good idea to have these posted somewhere in the room as a constant reminder throughout the school year of what is expected when your students are with you (Weinstein, 1996). Keep the list fairly simple; *no more than seven items* should be on this basic discipline guide. In addition, the consequences that you will employ if these rules are broken should be posted as well. Review Box 6.1 for a sample poster on classroom rules.

Box 6.1

SAMPLE POSTER: OUR CLASSROOM RULES

1. *Always be prepared for class!*

2. Be on time. (Refer to your syllabus for the tardy policy.)

3. Respect one another and everyone's personal belongings.

4. *Listen* to the designated speaker.

5. Raise your hand if you want to share something.

6. *Remain in your seat until you are asked to move.*

7. Use classroom equipment carefully, and *always* return items to their proper location.

Rewards

Make sure your students understand that these guidelines are to help everyone take advantage of the valuable learning time in the classroom (Jensen & Kiley, 2000). Let them know that if they'll cooperate, you'll be happy to reward them accordingly. Go over some of the positive rewards that you have planned for excellent behavior. In addition to good citizenship grades, you may give daily treats, table rewards, bonus points, free time, or even a movie or game day now and then. Some teachers even have their students work towards treats like a pizza day once a month or a free period outside playing baseball or some other game.

Although there is some criticism about rewarding students in these tangible ways, I have never come across a child (or an adult, for that matter) who wasn't willing to improve behavior if there was some positive reinforcement as a goal. Think about what type of system would work best for you and your particular group of students. You can modify this reward plan as you get more ideas from other teachers at your school, and your students will gladly supply you with their own suggestions!

Consequences

When students *do* start testing your classroom rules (they wouldn't be normal kids if they didn't try to pull something over on you within the first few weeks of school), make sure that you are consistent about reinforcing your established plan. If you fail to follow through, you will begin to lose the students' respect immediately (Wong & Wong, 1998). *Reinforce all behavior—good and bad—with the appropriate, pre-established reward or consequence.* Students will quickly learn that you mean business, and many will refrain from testing the rules again. It is far better to deal with these unpleasantries early on rather than letting things go and then trying to reign in student behavior midway through the year. Believe it or not, you will show the students how much you really do care when you establish firm boundaries that are for everyone's benefit!

THE FIRST DAY, WEEK, AND MONTH

Information Overload

As I've mentioned, the first day of school will be full of explanations and activities that will help acquaint everyone with the expectations of the upcoming year. Sometimes this can seem like "information overload" (for you as well as your students), so you may have to repeat or review many of these items again and again during the beginning weeks of school. Be patient when students ask you to re-explain what you've already stated. It usually means that they couldn't absorb all of the details the first time around. Once a few weeks have gone by, the students will be able to handle the schedule, class activities, homework, and all of your expectations with relative ease.

Forms and Paperwork

Your administrator will probably have a lot of paperwork for you to pass out to the students during these initial days. There are many forms that need to be completed by the parents and returned to the school office as quickly as possible. Often the first period or homeroom teacher is responsible for distributing and collecting these items. Whatever you do, don't lose these important documents! Many of the forms take parents several hours to fill out, and you don't want to begin the school year by telling them that they've got to redo something! Keep track of who has turned in what (you can use your grade book or class roster to check off all the returned paperwork), and remind students regularly about getting the required items back to school. Certain documents, such as those with medical information and emergency phone numbers, could be needed immediately!

Reflection: Start Early and Do It Often

At the end of the first day, spend some time reflecting on how your classes went. This is an excellent habit to establish early in your career. Ask yourself what made the events and activities successful. Was there anything that didn't go according to plan? How could you improve upon the lesson? Was there a way to respond to a situation more efficiently or effectively? Were there things that you didn't accomplish that you should add to tomorrow's lesson plans? Don't get discouraged if things didn't start out perfectly—they rarely do, even for those who've spent years in the classroom. In fact, many teachers will tell you that their best lessons came after failures. By reflecting on what *not* to do, we seem to learn the optimal methods to implement as we strive toward becoming exceptional educators.

After several weeks go by, you should have the basic procedures of your class well established and the curriculum underway. Now you will be able to get a feel for your students' ability levels and learning styles, as well as any personality, social, or emotional aspects that may require some intervention. If you see any glaring discrepancies in a student's performance or some type of red flag that raises your concern, take time to investigate this problem now. You may want to look at that student's cumulative file to see if your concerns are valid, or talk with the parent, school counselor, or an administrator to get additional input.

Think about setting aside 10 to 15 minutes at the end of every school day to analyze your lessons as well as all classroom interactions. Jot thoughts and ideas down in your plan book or journal so that you can follow up on ways to improve the situation. Be proactive! If you see something that needs adjusting, take action now.

The steps that you take during this first month of your new journey will help ensure that you experience success—both now and for the remainder of the school year.

Tips to Remember

1. If you know that behavior and classroom management are not your forte, then invest time studying ways to become more skilled in this vital aspect of the educational process. Most colleges and universities will have helpful texts in their schools of education or main library.

2. Keep a notepad by your teaching area so that you can write down new ideas to implement as they come to you. If you wait until the end of the school day, you may forget something fabulous that you wanted to try out with your class.

3. Attend workshops on classroom management and new instructional ideas that your district may offer. There are always innovations in teaching that you may not have been trained in. Be sure to keep track of the time you spend for your professional growth records (more information on this in Chapter 9).

4. Spend some time thinking (and maybe writing in your journal) about your role as an authority figure. What does this mean? How is this different from being the student's friend? How do you plan to balance earning the respect of students with maintaining a well-disciplined classroom environment?

7

Keeping the Records Straight

The history books are full of stories of gifted persons whose talents were overlooked by a procession of people until someone believed in them. Einstein was four years old before he could speak and seven before he could read. Isaac Newton did poorly in grade school. A newspaper editor fired Walt Disney because he had "no good ideas." Leo Tolstoy flunked out of college. . . . Haydn gave up ever making a musician of

"You play favorites — you give the best grades to the kids who study!"

Beethoven who seemed "a low and plodding young man with no apparent talent . . ."

—A. L. McGinnis

STUDENT EVALUATION AND MOTIVATION

Now that you've started out on this amazing adventure, it's time to develop a system for grading your students. Each of us can attest to the fact that the main reason for working is to make money, although there are other positive rewards as well. But, let's face it, if we toiled and labored for weeks and then were told that we wouldn't be paid, most of us would be extremely unhappy—to say the least! Even the adventurers who struggle up Mount Everest have the potential prize of reaching the peak. Deep within the core of the human spirit lies an intense desire to be recognized when we've exerted tremendous effort toward our goals.

This is as true for kids as it is for adults. Although students don't receive a paycheck, they like their labors to be acknowledged, especially by their parents and teachers. Youngsters are thrilled with stickers and smiley faces, while older learners strive to earn those A's and B's—and every student appreciates a simple "good job" from time to time (Weinstein, 1996). If you haven't given much thought to your system for evaluating your students' progress, now is certainly the time to do so. As we head out on the next leg of the educational journey, reflect back on how you felt about the rewards and recognition that you received in school. Were these motivational methods clear and consistent? How fair do you think the process was for *all* of the young people involved? As we shall see, this simple yet essential aspect of the educational system can either help to engage students or estrange them from the learning process.

SETTING UP YOUR GRADING SYSTEM

Power and Responsibility

One reason many people choose this profession is the freedom that they have to implement their own ideas and style within the classroom. As the teacher, you are in charge of everything from the seating arrangements to behavior management. The same is true for grading procedures, but with this liberty comes much responsibility. *The marks that you give to students are very personal to them.* Sometimes these grades can make the difference between children believing that they can do something or feeling like they are dismal failures. I'm sure you can think of scenarios during your own educational experience where you weren't rewarded appropriately for the time and effort that you put forth. Perhaps a teacher seemed to have it in for you, so that, no matter how hard you tried, you simply couldn't get an "A" on anything! What I'm trying to convey is that you are now in an *extremely powerful position!* In a sense, you are the "power broker" of the classroom. Please take time to carefully consider how you can utilize this authority to accentuate the academic success of all of your students.

Standards

In addition, you need to consider the standards that have been established by your state/district/school for the subject(s) that you are teaching. There has been a large movement in the United States to set up clear, defined expectations for learning across the curriculum and at every grade level (Spring, 1998). Some school districts have taken it upon themselves to write their own guidelines, while others have adopted state and national designs. It is quite possible that there is a "standards notebook" or similar resource that you should have, whether or not your administrator brought it to your attention. Although you do have a great deal of leeway in how you teach, these standards will explicitly define what you must cover in the curriculum as well as what the students will be expected to know once they exit your class. Furthermore, there is a growing correlation of the subject area content and performance standards to what will be on the tests given by your district and/or state (Jensen & Kiley, 2000; Spring, 1998).

Grading Methods

Since you have spent a great deal of time observing in a variety of classrooms in the past, you should have some good ideas on what grading method will complement your teaching style. Spend an evening or two outlining your ideas, and then revisit them after a few days have passed to be sure that this system satisfies your needs. Be certain to specify every detail—including how you will grade daily assignments, weekly work, projects, quizzes, tests, class participation, and citizenship. Will you give pluses, checks, and minuses on in-class material? Will homework be graded on an established point system based on how many problems were given? Do you plan to score everything as it comes in, or will students accumulate assignments in a notebook that you'll collect periodically for assessment purposes?

Although this process may seem tedious, defining these details now will save you a lot of time and trouble later on. For one thing, your students will immediately want to know how you will be grading their work. In addition, your principal as well as the parents will be keeping a close eye on your system for evaluating the learners. There's nothing more unprofessional than someone who is uncertain about a major aspect of her or his job. What if you went to a bank to ask about a loan and the employee said, "Sorry, I'm still trying to figure that out!" I bet you'd be looking for another banker immediately. Develop a specific plan for grading, and review it carefully before implementation. You may even want to have a colleague look it over to avoid any glitches. Once you've got this important piece of classroom operation down, you'll be ready to start the real job you prepared for: teaching your students!

ALTERNATIVE ASSESSMENT

As we discussed in Chapter 5, today's classrooms are full of diverse learners. In addition to rich ethnic backgrounds, our students also have an enormous array of gifts, talents, and special needs. Sadly, many of the methods that have been employed for decades in educational institutions seem to work best for only a small percentage of students (Darling-Hammond, 1997; Nieto, 2000). Indeed, most of our curriculum as well as assessment tools and techniques are strongly Western European in nature and often geared toward high achievers (Garcia, 1994).

As a new educator, you have the opportunity to dramatically change this situation. You can transform traditional teaching styles and methods of assessment to increase the chances for all children to acquire the information they need to be successful in school and in society (Banks, 1994). An optimal approach is to provide a wider variety of activities to determine whether or not the students have learned what you've been teaching. Rather than constantly testing to check for knowledge acquisition, you can offer the students the opportunity to *show what they know*. This is also referred to as "authentic assessment" (McNeil, 1996). Below are some ideas that you could utilize in any classroom in lieu of an exam (Armstrong, 2000; Garcia, 1994):

Fifteen Alternative Assessments Your Students Can Use

In lieu of an exam, your students can

1. Write a report
2. Make a scrapbook
3. Put on a demonstration for the class
4. Create group projects
5. Do statistical charts or diagrams
6. Paint a picture or mural
7. Design a game
8. Set up an experiment
9. Teach the class
10. Present a musical or play
11. Keep a journal
12. Develop a computer program
13. Formulate a problem-solving technique
14. Choreograph a dance
15. Interview an expert in the field

The list of alternative activities for today's learners goes on and on. Talk to your colleagues, and observe other classes on occasion to get new ideas. Your administrator may even provide release time for you to do this. Check out a book on alternative assessment, or attend a workshop that's offered on this topic. Many of the cutting-edge concepts come from teachers just like you who are trying new methods of assessing students. Keep an eye out for information in your faculty mailbox that may provide opportunities for you to learn something new.

Most important, be sure your students understand what these alternative assessments really mean. Explain the kinds of activities that they can do in detail. Ask them for suggestions on how these projects could be done, and even work together to plan a grading scale for them (see next section for further ideas). As they present what they've done, take pictures or video for future classes. Remember that you are acquiring better teaching skills as you watch your students share their knowledge in these alternative ways.

MORE IDEAS TO CONSIDER

During your university work or student teaching, you may have discovered that educators are implementing two innovations in grading. Although some teachers will tell you that they've been using them for years, the concepts of *rubrics and portfolios* are certainly new to many professionals in this field. Basically, a rubric is a numbered grading scale, as opposed to the traditional A, B, C system, while the portfolio method is a means of gathering information that actively involves students in the learning process (Jensen & Kiley, 2000).

Rubrics

A rubric typically is set up on a numbered scale. For example, a score of 1 (or even 0) could be given as the lowest score possible, while a 6 might represent outstanding achievement. Rubrics have descriptors assigned to each number that fully explain what the student has to do to achieve that mark. Let's say a writing assignment is given in a history class. The descriptor for a 6 might be something like this: "The essay is at least one full page in length, has no grammar or spelling errors, is creative in approach, and stays on the topic assigned." The descriptors for the other scores would reflect less fulfillment of the expectations for a "6" on this particular assignment.

One interesting aspect of rubrics is that the students can help the teacher design them! Indeed, this is a potential benefit of this unique approach to grading—student involvement as well as a feeling of ownership in the process. For instance, in a fourth-grade class, the teacher and students can discuss the criteria for evaluating an upcoming project on the mission buildings scattered throughout California. Class members can give input as to what the teacher should be looking for in terms of quality, effort, and completion of the task. The teacher can write students' ideas on the board or on an overhead, and then transfer these to an actual rubric form that he or she can use during the grading process.

Some schools and districts now use a rubric system for report cards. This is more often the case at the elementary level, since both parents and students typically prefer traditional grades for middle and high school. Although there are a few critics who say that a rubric score is just another way of representing an A, B, or C, many educators now feel that it is the actual detailed descriptors that make a positive difference in how students perform on various assignments. As the expectations are clearly defined and explained in the rubric system, students can clearly see what is required, rather than trying to fulfill a teacher's subjective system or to do "the best they can" to receive an ambiguous grade. And research definitely shows that grades must reflect specific criteria to have a successful impact on student learning (Wong & Wong, 1998).

Portfolios and Student Work Samples

The use of portfolios has also grown from a classroom to a districtwide movement for gathering information in a wide range of disciplines, for teachers as well as for students (Lyons, 1998). In a portfolio—which basically starts as an empty file folder or binder—students save samples of their work over time. Sometimes the papers have already been scored, and the students have the chance to collect the best examples of what they've done so far in the class. Portfolios can also be used to show growth over time, so the teacher might direct the students to select a variety of projects and assignments for review at the end of the semester or school year.

For example, in a math class, a teacher could ask students to save items from the first month of school up until the next grading period. As the time for report cards approaches, the students could then be directed to survey their collection of work and write a one-page summary about how they feel they've progressed so far. At this point, the teacher would gather all of the portfolios for assessment. With the availability of technology, some teachers are now using "electronic portfolios" where the students merely turn in a disc for grading (Jensen & Kiley, 2000).

Some districts are now requiring portfolios in many subject areas. For instance, English teachers will pass on the eighth-grade folder to the freshman English teachers at the high school so they can look them over during the summer and use them as they prepare for their courses. These portfolios continue to move with the students from grade to grade until they became part of the graduation review process. In other words, seniors have to show a large collection of their writing in the portfolio in order to receive their diplomas.

Of course there are still skeptics of this method of assessment. Some educators wonder whether the next teacher will actually take time to review the materials that they've worked so hard to collect. Others are concerned with the practical aspects of this assessment technique, for instance, where will all of these portfolios be stored from year to year? If you consider a large public high school that may have 1,000 incoming freshmen who each have English, math, history, and science portfolios, you can understand the immensity of this problem!

Yet it has become obvious to many educators across the country that the utilization of portfolios and rubrics is another example of how students can become actively engaged in learning. As they spend time gathering, organizing, and analyzing their work, the students will actually be able to track their own progress and begin to evaluate how much the educational process is impacting their lives.

THE GRADE BOOK

Now we're ready to discuss what you probably thought would be the opening subject of this chapter—the grade book itself.

Although I know how important tracking grades is in our profession, I believe the other concepts we have discussed are far more essential to consider as you begin to think about how you will reward your students for their efforts!

Once you've discovered a system that works for you, you'll have no trouble purchasing or designing a tool where you can record your students' grades. After obtaining a satisfactory grade book, you simply begin by inputting your students' names alphabetically; you can then record each assignment with the specific scores in columns that correspond with the names (Wong & Wong, 1998).

As you are also probably aware, there are a number of quality software programs on the market that you can use on your school and/or home computer. Some school sites will offer training on these systems as well as free software products. You can also check with your school secretary, the district office, or even the county office of education for classes on computerized grading if you need assistance. These computer programs can print out a variety of reports on students' progress with the touch of a button. The downfall, as with many electronic devices, is the potential for loss, damage, or theft! If you choose to use a computer grading system, I strongly recommend that you keep some type of hard copy of the grades that you've recorded as well as an electronic backup file. Many teachers will use a traditional grade book as their hard copy, and then enter these scores into their computer.

Keep It Current

Be sure you are keeping current with the grading that needs to be done for your classes. It is so easy to get busy and fall behind on paperwork—until one day you find a mountain of reports, essays, and tests flowing off your desk. A professional works to stay current with the tasks at hand, and, for teachers, this includes the mundane job of grading and recording papers. In addition, students need to see the results of their work as quickly as possible, and some of them will begin to bug you if items are not returned within a reasonable time period. Rapid turnaround is better for the students because it gives them prompt feedback as well as an immediate reward for their efforts.

Part of your job during the first few months of school is to come up with a schedule that will work effectively in terms of planning, preparing, and grading. This may take time to figure out, but don't lose heart! Many educators spend countless late nights and weekends grading during their first year or two of teaching until they discover a method that is faster and more efficient. Talk to other teachers in your subject area or grade level if you are struggling!

Keep It Useful

As the year goes on, you will discover that your grade book can be a useful tool for a variety of things. The first page or two will probably hold your attendance records; the other pages will be filled with students' names and their corresponding grades. Be sure to label each page with the course title, class period, and the current semester that it reflects. Administrators will occasionally ask to see how you keep track of these records when they come to observe. In addition, you can use the grade book when you talk to parents during conferences or make a phone call about missing work. Also, students should be able to sit down with you at any time to discuss their progress as well as any concerns they have about their posted grades.

Just as your paycheck is essential to you, pupils value every mark, smiley face, sticker, and comment that you place on their papers. For some of them, these are the only positive rewards that they receive in life. Whatever system you choose to establish, it must be fair, easily understood, and accessible to everyone involved in the learning process. The ideas about grading that you had as a student teacher may change now that you have your own classroom, and that's okay! Use this year to try out your own concepts as well as glean as many new ones as you can from other educators. Eliminate anything that does not work with your style, students, or courses, and seek help when you're stuck. As time goes by, you'll become an expert at keeping your records straight!

Tips to Remember

1. Ask your school administrators if they provide teachers with a grade book. Like the plan book, if you don't like this one, visit a teacher supply store for other styles that might better meet your needs—or design one of your own.

2. Make an overhead that explains your grading system and use it sometime during the first week of school. Have students calculate a few examples—such as a student with all his homework assignments turned in versus one who completes only half of them. By doing this, they can see the importance of turning in all of their work!

3. Check out a book on alternative assessment, or attend a workshop on innovative evaluation techniques. Never get stuck using one style of grading. We always have room for improvement in the field of educating young minds!

4. Store all of your old grade books and records some place safe after the school year is over. You never know when a grade may be questioned or you might have to give feedback on a particular student several years down the road.

8

The People You'll Meet Along the Way

I attribute the little I know to my not having been ashamed to ask for information and to my rule of conversing with all descriptions of men on those topics that form their own peculiar profession and pursuits.

—John Locke

"Pay attention—today's lesson is the most important thing you'll ever learn in Drivers Education Class!"

Wherever you've traveled in life, you've probably come across a wide variety of people on your journey. On our populous planet, it's hard not to bump into someone even while taking a quiet stroll or sitting beside a cool stream. Part of the fun of traveling is getting to meet interesting folks from all corners of our globe. This is also true of the teaching experience. As you enter your new career, you will soon discover the important role that other individuals will play in your classroom successes.

Although some consider the job of a teacher to be a solitary one, I'm sure you've already observed just how inaccurate this assumption truly is. Besides the numerous students you will come in contact with on a daily basis, there will be many adults who contribute to your professional experiences. As in any business, these colleagues will be essential to the development of your career. From the very first moment that you meet someone, consider how he or she may impact your career, not only now, but also in the future.

For instance, the mentor teacher that assists you during your first year on the job may one day provide a recommendation that could lead to another position in the future. Years ago I was hired by a school district closer to my home because the principal was a friend of my former administrator. Although I still had to prove I merited the position, the final recommendation of this colleague sealed the deal. A student teacher that I worked with was offered a contract upon graduation because everyone, from the secretarial staff to the custodian, raved about her professionalism and courtesy on campus.

As we make a quick analysis of some of the key people you will be working with over the course of your profession, I want to again remind you how crucial these initial impressions can be. When you meet new people, be polite, courteous, and professional. Make a point to learn the person's name—especially the correct pronunciation. You might even make notes in your plan book of this individual's name, what position he or she has in your school or district, and any other essential data that you might need to recall later. Some of these colleagues may cross your path only on occasion, while others will be part of your everyday experience.

SCHOOL ADMINISTRATORS

Among those who will be your supervisors in the teaching profession are superintendents, principals, and assistant principals (sometimes called "vice principals"). More than likely, you have met several of these leaders through the interview and hiring process. If not, be sure to find out who they are and introduce yourself. They need to get to know you so that, at the end of the year, you will have a greater chance of being asked to teach for them again!

Although many new teachers in large districts don't have the opportunity to regularly interact with the superintendent, you should still be familiar with who he/she is in case there is a surprise visit to your campus. Some districts have introductory luncheons or other meetings where you can meet the superintendent and other prominent district personnel. I suggest that you attend as many of these functions as possible.

Supervision, Evaluation, and Classroom Observation

Your principal or one of the assistant principals will be responsible for your formal evaluations during your first year of teaching. You will also be observed on a regular basis by some type of supervisor during your second year of teaching, which is a standard procedure before any teacher becomes tenured. Even after the tenure status is attained, most districts require regular observations of the teaching staff by supervisors, although it may change to a biyearly evaluation at that point in your career. This process involves several scheduled visits by the evaluator during the course of the school year. The evaluator will watch you work during one full class period to see how you interact with the students, to review your lesson plans and teaching methodology, and to get an overall feel for your effectiveness in an educational setting.

Although these supervisors may drop in unannounced from time to time, most of them will set up formal appointments for observations. Just as you prepared for your student teaching supervisor's visits, you should take time to design a thorough lesson with a *typed plan* for him/her to follow. Also, make sure that he/she has a copy of the textbook as well as any other materials that you will be utilizing with your students (worksheets, directions for a hands-on activity, etc.).

Try to act as normally as possible (which, I realize, is easier said than done). All of these evaluators were in a similar situation at one time in their careers, so they understand what you are going through. Depending on how you think your students may react to a guest in the classroom, you may decide it's best to talk to them about this visit beforehand. I often told my classes that the principal or assistant principal would be stopping by to observe "us" and to find out how things were going in our classroom. This usually helped my students be on their best behavior! The rest was up to me!

Mentoring, Support, and Assistance

In addition to his or her role in the evaluation process, your principal is also someone to seek out when you have questions on anything related to your school or teaching practice. Don't try to handle everything on your own, especially if classroom management, student concerns, or parental problems escalate to a level that requires additional intervention. Yet, realistically, every school has its own culture and working climate. If you are uncertain of the best direction to take when dealing with certain problems at your school site, ask a co-worker you trust for help. Sometimes fellow teachers are the safest source to answer your specific questions. Also, many school districts now provide mentor teachers to support new educators. Most important, don't be afraid to reach out to someone to get assistance as well as show that you are willing to participate in the overall school community (Jensen & Kiley, 2000).

TEACHING COLLEAGUES AND TEACHER LEADERS

In some teaching positions, you may be asked to work directly with one or more of your colleagues. Even if you are not in a cooperative teaching setting, all educators should picture themselves as part of the entire school "team." During the course of this first year, you will meet many staff members at your site. Try to get to know as many of them as possible, for they truly are your fellow travelers in this educational journey (Wong & Wong, 1998). It's nice to be able to greet someone in the hall or lunchroom by his or her first name. Be sure to reintroduce yourself if it seems that someone has forgotten who you are, and don't take it personally! Some campuses have 50 or more people on staff, so it may take time for them to get to know you.

The certificated staff members are fellow teachers, counselors, and librarians (more on the last two in the next section); you will more than likely have the most direct and daily contact with these individuals. You may have to report to some of these professionals for various aspects of your job. For example, department chairs or team leaders will schedule meetings, make curriculum suggestions, and provide inservices on new district guidelines.

It is crucial that you, the "new kid on the block," learn how to work with these key people. Not only will the administrator ask for their feedback from time to time on how you are progressing, but they also may be questioned at the end of the year about whether or not you should continue to be part of the permanent faculty. No matter what role these certificated personnel have on your campus, they are fellow professionals and should be treated with the utmost respect. Attaining the invaluable input and ideas that these "teacher leaders" have to offer will enhance your blossoming skills as well as improve the overall educational experience for the students in your classroom (Jensen & Kiley, 2000).

SUPPORT STAFF

In addition to administrators, fellow teachers, and counselors, there is a wide array of support staff on each campus. Many of these people will be extremely helpful to you on a daily basis. As with all other professional contacts, try to make a good first impression. Introduce yourself when you come across someone you have not met before. If you have questions, don't be shy about asking the support staff for assistance. That's why they are at your school—to support you and the students!

Administrative Staff

The administrative staff in the main office is usually the most visible extra support at your site. These people include the school secretary(ies), the attendance clerk(s), and other aides that help oversee the daily functions of the school. Many of these staff members will be the ones who get you started when you show up that very first day. They'll assign you a room key, show you around the campus, and assist you in locating items like supplies, textbooks, forms—even a cup of coffee!

Custodial Staff

When I started teaching, an experienced teacher on campus told me that the one person I should make friends with was the school custodian. Of course, I thought my new friend was exaggerating. *The custodian?* Why on earth would I want to worry about getting to know him? (By the way, some years it was a her!) It didn't take long for me to find out. Two days before school started I didn't have any trashcans—and there was an acrid odor in my room that was beginning to chase the flies away! Whom did I call? You bet—the custodian. He appeared with the cans—as well as the largest can of room freshener I'd ever seen. He also located the dead mouse behind a file cabinet! Since that time, I have grown to respect the role these individuals play in keeping the appearance of our schools neat and orderly. They work extremely hard with little recognition, and I've learned a tremendous amount from their dedication and efforts on behalf of students.

Library Media Specialists

If you've not spent much time in the library on campus, try to fit in a visit during the first few weeks of school. You should get to know the school librarian as well as any other library support staff. Librarians themselves are certificated personnel who not only are well read, but also aware of a multitude of resources in the field of education. If your librarian doesn't have the exact book that you need, he/she may be able to track it down for you or find money in the budget to order it! At smaller schools, the librarians are sometimes in charge of the audiovisual equipment, or they might be the ones who order these materials from the district office.

School Counselors

Counselors usually assist in student placement, master planning, individual and group interventions, and supervision of many campus programs. At a smaller school, a counselor might only be available once a week because he/she travels from site to site. Larger campuses might have a counselor for each grade level. These are important people for you to become acquainted with because they can help you with questions or concerns about certain students, and they can attend parent conferences at your request. Be sure to become familiar with the procedure on your campus for sending students to talk to a counselor.

School Health, Safety, and Nutrition Experts

Other key staff members include the school nurse, the psychologist, the resource specialists, the speech therapist, the lunchroom workers, and the security personnel. Depending on the size of your school, you may have many names and faces to remember during this first year on the job. As you start to make connections with each person on campus, you will really begin to feel like a team player.

PARENTS AND GUARDIANS

You may not see or speak to the parents and/or guardians of your students every day, but you will—and should—do so from time to time. As you make contact with them, remember that they are a key connection to ensure that you and the students have a successful school year. These primary caregivers are the other educators of your students, and they have a major investment in all that you are doing for their children. Some of them will want to get involved (on a wide variety of levels), and many will desire to work collaboratively with you in the learning process (Jensen & Kiley, 2000; Weinstein, 1996).

During the first month of school, you will have the opportunity to meet at least one parent or guardian for each of your students. Some will stop by before school even begins to show their children the campus and your classroom. Even if this is an unexpected visit, be friendly and take time to greet them. Other parents will pop in on the first day of school to say hello. Most sites will have a "Back-to-School Night" sometime during the first few weeks of school; this might be your first opportunity to interact with parents and guardians. In addition to the school's official invitation to this event, you may want to send out your own notes of encouragement to attend this special evening, so these caregivers can meet you and become familiar with the plans that you have for their children during the school year.

A few caregivers may not be as friendly or interested in their children's education as we might like. For these individuals, you should place personal phone calls as soon as possible. As you meet and/or talk to each parent or guardian, make a mark of some type next to that student's name in your grade book to indicate that you've met with his or her caregiver. About the second or third week of school, check over this list. The students who have no marks next to their names should be the focus of your attention. Call their homes in the evening, or send a message through the school mail. Even if you only get an answering machine, at least you have made the effort to form a positive connection. I suggest trying to contact each and every parent or guardian early in the school year. The benefits of enlisting their support will help you in the days, weeks, and months ahead (Weinstein, 1996).

Remember, primary caregivers are the most important influences in your students' lives. They take care of "your kids" during the rest of the day and night. Most parents and guardians are very concerned about their children, and it is essential that we form strong connections with them to aid in the overall success of our students (Curwin & Mendler, 1999; Weinstein, 1996). They will want to hear from you when you need their assistance. Encourage them to be part of the learning community. Perhaps they can volunteer in your classroom or on campus in some capacity. Ask for their input and suggestions, and be sure to send lots of information home about what their children are learning and doing at school.

As you continue down the road of this exciting career, you'll soon learn that you are not alone on this educational journey. Some people will only join you for short jaunts while others may sojourn alongside you all the way to retirement. Enjoy each individual's unique personality and perspective, and try to glean as much as you can from these fellow travelers. Eventually you will have the privilege of returning the favor as you provide insights and advice to others you meet along the way who may just be beginning the journey.

Tips to Remember

1. Many schools have personnel directories with the names, addresses, and phone numbers of all staff members. Try to get a copy of this, and keep it in a safe place.

2. Make a file folder of notes, e-mails, or messages that you send to other staff members and parents. I recommend a "documentation" file for each year that you teach. This way, if there is ever a question about anyone you contacted regarding a specific concern, you will simply have to pull this file out for easy reference.

3. Sometimes staff members will move to other sites after several years at one school. Be sure to keep in contact with people that you feel have been and may continue to be important to your professional development!

4. It is essential that you return telephone, e-mail, and other messages in a prompt manner—usually *within 24 hours!* This courtesy to others will only add to your professional credibility.

9

Professional Development

Charting Your Progress

The educator believes in the worth and dignity of man. He recognizes the supreme importance of the pursuit of truth, devotion to excellence, and the nurture of democratic citizenship. He regards as essential to these goals the protection of freedom to learn and to teach and the guarantee of equal educational opportunities for all. The educator accepts his

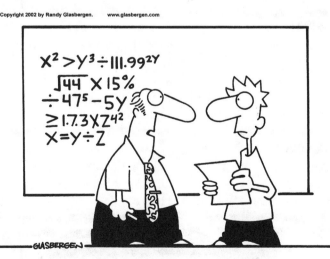

"Can you keep a secret? I've been teaching this
stuff for 15 years and I still don't understand it."

*responsibility to practice his profession according to the
highest ethical standards . . .*

—From the preamble of the National Education
Association Code of Ethics of the Education Profession

Teaching is a profession that requires constant growth,
especially since its primary goal is to impart the latest
information to the adults of tomorrow. With the knowledge base
continuing to expand at exponential rates, it is essential for educators to keep up with new innovations and ideas as well as methods
to make these concepts more accessible to all students. As a professional in this field, you can no longer rely on a standard textbook and traditional instructional techniques that worked
decades ago; instead, you must stay current on educational
research and be ready to adapt your teaching styles to best meet
the students' needs (Darling-Hammond et al., 1999; Wong &
Wong, 1998).

In addition, teachers must be aware of innovations in their
specialty area and keep updated on any new insights or ideas on
curriculum and instructional methods. All educators must also
meet certain professional standards to maintain their teaching
credential(s). Your state department of education will require you
to fulfill a number of requirements within a given time period after
you receive your initial credential. You may be asked to take an
additional course (or courses), attend seminars or workshops in
your subject area, or expand your knowledge in areas like diversity or language development via reading or travel.

This increased accountability is a significant development in
our profession. Most of us wouldn't want to go to a physician who
was not aware of the latest medical advancements or had failed to
attend a seminar that would improve his or her surgical techniques.
As you continue to travel down the educational highway, you'll
not only need to grow professionally in order to renew your credential, but you should also be aware of the numerous break-
throughs and exciting changes in your field in order to provide
your students with the optimum experience possible within your
classroom (Fullan, 1993; Jensen & Kiley, 2000).

PROFESSIONAL GROWTH

Teaching Credentials

As I mentioned, all states have some supervisory agency and process for monitoring the teaching profession. Although more effort is being made at the national level to establish a unified system of standards for educators, at this time each state has its own criteria for teachers to update and maintain their credentials (Darling-Hammond et al., 1999; Spring, 2002). Even though you typically will not have to renew your teaching credential for four or five years, you should have this information from your state agency so you can begin thinking about this process. If you didn't receive a guidebook or manual with your credential, then check with your school district's human resources department or call the state credentialing office to request that one be sent to you as soon as possible. Many of the seminars, workshops, professional activities, and college courses you participate in over the next few years must be documented with complete accuracy for you to receive credit in this renewal process.

Professional Development Plans (PDPs)

In order to maintain your credential, you will be asked to design a professional development plan (PDP). PDPs involve the goals and objectives, methods and materials, and the rationales involved in your teaching experiences (Jensen & Kiley, 2000). For example, during the course of a semester, you may want to increase your knowledge about Attention-Deficit/Hyperactivity Disorder (ADHD) because you have a student in your class who has this condition. You may choose to read a book, take a class, attend a seminar, or spend time talking to experts like the school psychologist to learn more about how to meet these special needs. The goal you've set (for example, "improve my knowledge of ADHD"), the actions that you take to meet this goal, and the time involved in the actual activity should be documented in your PDP. Many states have required forms to use for the PDP, but you may choose to keep your own form or even a computer file with more detailed information. If you attend a class or workshop, keep the handouts or workbooks you receive for future reference as well as for proof that the activity met your pre-established goal.

Professional Development Activities

Whatever you do, document all professional development activities. A sample log that you can begin on your own is shown in Table 9.1. In order to develop as a professional in the field of education, you must to set your own goals and make plans to work on these specific areas of growth. Your supervisor or mentor teacher can also suggest areas to focus on during your first year in the classroom. Keep in mind that professional growth should be a delightful process and not something that you dread. An exciting aspect of teaching is that you can always learn, change, take risks, and stretch yourself in ways that you never dreamed possible.

ORGANIZING ALL THOSE ORGANIZATIONS

Just as lawyers, nurses, businessmen, and doctors have their own professional groups, educators have a wide variety of associations that they can join as well. Although the decision to become a member of an educational organization is personal, I would challenge you to investigate the numerous options available to you and consider selecting at least one to become involved with during the course of your career. The reasons for this include the following:

1. Being part of a professional group will assist you in keeping up on the latest information, ideas, and techniques in your specialty area as well as in the field of education in general.

2. Membership in these types of organizations will allow you to meet and form contacts with other educators who can offer advice, insight, and opportunities to enhance your professional development.

3. Many organizations offer educational journals that will help you stay current on the latest research as well as glean new ideas to incorporate into your classroom.

Teacher Unions

One of the first options that you will encounter as a new teacher is whether or not to join a teacher's union. There are two major organizations for educators in the United States: the

Table 9.1

Professional Growth Activities

Type of Activity	Date / Time Involved	Goals Addressed
1. Workshop on district reading program	8/26/02 (2 hours)	Knowledge of student literacy needs.
2. Cultural competency meeting	9/17/02 (3 hours)	Increase understanding of diversity issues on my campus.
3. Two day class on cooperative learning	10/24/02 & 10/25/02 (14 hours)	Acquire new skills for helping all students become successful in my classroom.
4. Attended local harvest festival	10/31/02 (1.5 hours)	Get involved in school and community to increase awareness of local culture.
5. Read book on alternative assessment	11/5/02 – 1/15/03 (10 hours)	Acquire new skills for helping all students become successful in my classroom.
6. Helped on spelling bee committee	2/4/03& 2/21/03 (3.5 hours)	Improve knowledge of student literacy needs.
7. Assisted with Spring dance	3/28/03 (4 hours)	Get involved in school and community to increase awareness of local culture.
8. Joined multicultural committee	(Should begin in April, 2003)	Increase understanding of diversity issues on my campus.

National Education Association (NEA) and the American Federation of Teachers (AFT). Both groups have branches at the state and local levels. Some new teachers have concerns about associating themselves with a union because they have not been tenured yet, or perhaps they are uncertain of the political affiliations of the association.

Unfortunately, some educators and many people in the general public have misconceptions about the historical significance as well as current importance of teacher unions. I will give you a brief overview of both of these organizations, but I recommend that you investigate the local union that represents the teachers in your district and consider whether it meets your professional and personal needs.

The NEA was founded in 1857 in order to bring several education associations in the United States together. During the 19th and early 20th centuries, this new organization had a major influence in shaping the development of public schools. The NEA also played a role in standardizing teacher training in America. Until the 1960s, the majority of its membership consisted of superintendents, college professors, and administrators (Spring, 2002).

During the 1960s and 1970s, the NEA focused on teacher welfare and government lobbying. Many believe that the influence of the NEA has resulted in increased power and prestige for classroom teachers. Currently, the NEA remains very politically active, and it heartily supports many pro-education politicians (Johnson, Dupuis, Musial, Hall, & Gollnick, 2002).

The American Federation of Teachers (AFT) began in 1897 as part of a struggle by female grade-school teachers to attain adequate pension laws in Illinois. Its early efforts centered on retirement issues and teacher salaries. The AFT utilized a style similar to the labor movements in addressing teacher welfare issues as well as improving public education. Although the AFT originally had a no-strike policy, after the successful use of a "work stoppage" with the Buffalo, New York, Teachers Federation in 1947, the AFT began to change its practices. During this strike for higher salaries, other local unions supported the teachers; in fact, local drivers delivered only enough fuel to the schools to keep the pipes from freezing. This strike in Buffalo later served as a model for labor actions by teachers' unions across the country (Spring, 2002).

The AFT has also been concerned about greater teacher participation in the control of schools; its members have always felt that professionals in the classroom should have a voice and be able to vote on educational policies. As early as 1912, the AFT demanded an end to sexism in education. Like the NEA, the AFT grew rapidly in size, membership, and power between the 1960s and 1980s. This association is affiliated with the American Federation of Labor and Congress of Industrial Organizations (AFL-CIO), so it will implement strikes as well as utilize collective bargaining to fight for the welfare of educators in the United States (Johnson et al., 2002; Spring, 2002).

Teaching Associations

There are also a variety of other professional organizations for you to select from in the field of education. For example, the Association for Supervision and Curriculum Development (ASCD) is a national organization that publishes books, supplementary materials, and journals on numerous educational topics; it also provides workshops, seminars, and conferences where world-renowned speakers share research on effective classroom practices. The American Educational Research Association (AERA) is another national group that supports professionals in the field of education. It also offers annual conferences on the latest in educational research.

In addition, there are associations for educators to join in their specific credential or specialty area. For instance, you can find an organization just for math, science, English, or social studies teachers, or there are groups for those who work in elementary, middle-school, and high-school settings. These professional organizations offer support and up-to-date information on the specific subject areas. Most of these associations will also provide monthly, quarterly, and annual publications with current research as well as practical ideas and advice from other professionals in the field. Talk to your colleagues about what organizations they have been most satisfied with over the years, and don't forget to search the Internet for additional ideas.

PROFESSIONAL DEVELOPMENT ACTIVITIES

Whether or not you belong to a teacher's union or other association, it is essential that you become involved in activities within your profession. One benefit of this type of participation is that you will meet other educators whose professional and personal qualities will be an asset to you, especially during the first few years of teaching. It is also essential that you have the support of other individuals who have gone through, or are going through, some of the same situations that you will be confronting in and out of the classroom. Although there are people who think of teaching as an individual journey, this is far from the truth. We need the guidance and encouragement of our colleagues and co-workers as we strive to live up to the incredible role that we have assumed.

Opportunities at Your School

What kinds of professional activities are available to you? First, begin by looking at your own school site. As soon as the school year starts, there will be opportunities for you to become involved on campus. You could sponsor a student group or help with a school-wide project. Maybe you can coach a sport that you participated in when you were in school. There will be committees that need your assistance and expertise. Perhaps your background is in literature, and your school is trying to improve its literacy program. Find out who is in charge of this effort and offer your services. Remember, your involvement also shows administrators that you are trying to be a team player on campus.

Opportunities in Your School District

Second, investigate opportunities for involvement at the district level. Most district offices offer inservices, workshops, and seminars throughout the school year that are free of charge to employees. Keep your eye out for fliers in your mailbox or posted in the faculty lounge. If you are interested in a particular subject, contact the district office to ask about upcoming conferences or special events. There are also districtwide committees you can join. Talk to your principal if you would like to become involved outside of the campus; he or she should have more information about these opportunities.

Opportunities for Long-Term Career Growth

In addition to noting them on your PDP, you will also want to add many of these activities to your résumé. As you begin to make connections with other professionals in the field, keep these people in mind for potential references. Be aware that certain travel experiences can often be part of a PDP. Review your guidebook for credential renewal about specific criteria regarding this, and ask your co-workers about how they've used vacations to work on their professional goals (more on travel experiences in Chapter 11).

Teachers need to enter this vocation with the understanding that completing college is only the *beginning* of the educational journey. *Teaching is more than a job; it is a profession in process.* Acquiring new information and ideas doesn't end when you sign your first contract, get tenured, complete five years of teaching, or earn another graduate degree. Learning is a lifelong experience. Even though we may be mandated by our state to meet certain requirements, all of us should experience the joy and exhilaration of keeping our skills sharp for our benefit as well as our students'! And, finally, don't worry about what everyone else is doing; just get going—and keep growing!

Tips to Remember

1. Be careful not to become over-ambitious when it comes to setting goals. Try to choose *three or four main areas* that you'd like to focus on during the first year or two of teaching. You'll have many years ahead of you to work on your growth as a professional.

2. Even if your state does not require it, find an advisor to help you with your PDP. This should be an experienced teacher, mentor, or administrator who can assist as you set specific goals and give you ideas on how to complete them within a reasonable period of time.

3. Subscribe to at least one educational journal so that you can think about new concepts, read encouraging stories, and delve into the latest research in your subject area. Your school, district, or university library will also have many educational periodicals for you to peruse.

10

Staying on Track Throughout the School Year

Always bear in mind that your own resolution to succeed is more important than any other one thing.

—Abraham Lincoln

"This is the finest, most comprehensive and informative term paper I've ever read. But you were supposed to write about 'Plato' not 'Playdough'."

After a successful start to your school year, you should be able to face the future with increased confidence. It takes a tremendous amount of time, talent, energy, and effort to get any class up and running. Now that your students know more about you, your expectations, the class rules, and the direction that the curriculum will take in the coming months, they should be willing to follow your lead down the pathway of learning (Weinstein, 1996; Wong & Wong, 1998). You should also feel more secure in your new position since you've become familiar with your students, their parents, and your colleagues. The challenge that lies ahead is to maintain this forward motion while enjoying the process of teaching your students!

Unfortunately, some teachers make a critical error at this point in the year regarding the classroom environment. They often assume that once they have laid the groundwork for success, the rest of the pieces of the educational process will somehow fall into place. This is like a construction crew pouring a cement floor, then hoping that the beams, walls, and roof will magically fall into their correct position. Ridiculous? You bet! And so is the wishful thinking of some would-be educators that starting out strong will automatically ensure a fantastic finish. Not only is this unrealistic, but it also goes against the very forces of nature. After all, the Second Law of Thermodynamics states that *all* things in the universe go from order to disorder unless energy is placed into the system! And we can definitely see this law at work in our classrooms!

A good start should provide the initial push that's needed to lead you toward a powerful finish, but you must continue to put forth effort and energy along the entire journey. Much of your time will be spent planning, and then trying to stick to the goals you've developed. Interruptions will come—assemblies, special events, testing, and even emergencies—but you can always go back to the plans you've prepared as well as your master calendar to get you back on track.

The ideas in the following sections are designed to give you an overview of what to expect during an average school year. The discussion follows the traditional school schedule of September through June, but the principles can be adapted to any type of calendar. Every school track, whether traditional or year-round, will have a "beginning" when the excitement and energy levels are high. This will be followed by the "middle of the year" season where the majority of the learning experience takes place. Finally, the crucial "end" of the calendar year will be upon you, with all of its culminating activities and preparations for the next grade or even graduation. Like the seasons themselves, the cycle of the school year has its own natural rhythm, and you will discover that there is much to accomplish during these upcoming months. If you're ready, let's take a look at what the days ahead have in store for you and the students.

OCTOBER TO DECEMBER: "GETTING IT GOING"

What an exhilarating time of year! Memories of summer vacations have faded, and your students are enjoying the wonderful classroom and engaging curriculum that you're providing for them. It's almost as if a cool autumn breeze has swept into all of your lives, leaving a sense of expectation in the air! The students have begun to make new friends and are feeling comfortable in the calm, caring environment that you've established. You've given them just enough hints about the future so they can hardly wait to find out what fun activities they'll get to do while acquiring so much new information.

These are the months during which you can easily hook most students into learning! They are ready to read and write, do arithmetic, and try a plethora of new things. Take advantage of their enthusiasm because this energized state could change at any moment! Check your plan book and master calendar to make certain that your academic goals are heavily stressed during the fall and early winter season.

Speaking of seasons, you will have numerous opportunities in the days ahead to incorporate cultural events and holidays into the curriculum. Elementary teachers are especially adept at incorporating pumpkins, Pilgrims, and brightly wrapped packages into the curriculum and onto bulletin boards during the months of October, November, and December. Sometimes middle- and high-school teachers forget how much fun these seasonal activities can be for the older students as well. Although you will be concentrating on academics, weave some celebrations and cultural themes throughout your lessons. Be sure to include many of the ethnic and cultural celebrations that occur during this season (for ideas on this, see Cech in Resource B, Recommended Readings). It's easy to work a special art activity or seasonal project into most subject areas. How about going outside and studying fall leaves for science? What about a pumpkin-decorating contest for art? For math, make up a worksheet and have the students calculate how much a farmer could earn with a particular crop during the harvest season.

These seasonal activities and celebrations add interest and diversity to an ordinary curriculum. It's also an excellent way to increase cultural connections in your classroom. Look for opportunities to learn more about the background of your students, and let them give you ideas on how to embrace and celebrate their heritage and culture. By doing so, your students will begin to appreciate their similarities and differences, as well as those of other people in the world. See Box 10.1 for a few ideas on celebrations that will get you started during the upcoming months.

In addition to these activities, be sure to design lessons that give your students the chance to get to know one another and feel like they are truly active members of the classroom experience. Spend one-on-one time with each student so you can develop a more personal connection with them as well. There's growing evidence that the reason some students don't do well in school is that they feel distant and disconnected from the learning experience (Banks, 1994; Darling-Hammond, 1997). Try to get kids working in groups to increase cooperation, communication, and collaboration as well as to build confidence (Johnson, Johnson, & Holubec, 1994). As you begin to include these invaluable interactions within your classroom, you will find that the possibilities for future learning and success are endless!

JANUARY TO MARCH: "KEEPING IT GOING"

After the winter holidays are over, you and your students should feel refreshed—but not always ready to return to school. It's hard to see all of the fun and festivities of the previous season come to an end, and many of us wish we had another week or two to sleep in and relax. When you compound this melancholy mood with gray, misty mornings or frosty weather, no wonder we find it so difficult to return to the routine of the classroom!

Box 10.1

MULTICULTURAL CELEBRATIONS FOR THE
CLASSROOM

_____**OCTOBER:**   Harvest Festivals—celebrated
throughout the world during this
time of year (see Cech's *Globalchild*
in Resource B, Recommended
Reading)

National UNICEF Month (the United
Nations Children's Fund)

_____**NOVEMBER:**   Thanksgiving

_____**DECEMBER to JANUARY:**

Las Posadas

Christmas

Chanukah

Kwanzaa

"Festival of Lights" (look at
Globalchild for other suggestions on
these winter celebrations)

_____**FEBRUARY:**   African-American History Month

Chinese New Year

*For other ideas throughout the calendar year, see Tiedt &
Tiedt in Resource B, Recommended Reading.

Even if you are energized and excited about the educational goals and activities you've planned for the months of January, February, and March, realize that some—or many—of your students may not be so exuberant. In fact, that original enthusiasm that seemed to almost bounce off the walls at the start of the school year may be non-existent the first week after Winter Break. A new challenge awaits you: How can you reignite that fire for learning?

Although some educators often feel as if their role is one of ringleader in an educational circus, at times teachers really are like a master of ceremonies in the classroom. Since our students may not be interested in learning at the moment, we must creatively devise methods to capture their attention. This may mean starting off with a fun activity or project before focusing back on the hard-core academics. You might want to think about a field trip during the first week or two after the break so that you can spark interest in a new unit or theme. In physical education, the kids could come up with indoor activities for inclement weather, and then they can teach these to the rest of the class. In fact, letting the students take over at various times may be exactly what is needed during this season. How about breaking the students into groups, giving them some guidelines and expectations, and then let them take off with their own creativity and learning styles? After the allotted time is up, have them share their findings, results, or lessons with the larger group (Johnson, Johnson, & Holubec, 1994).

Remember to continue looking for seasonal ideas and cultural celebrations to include in your classroom experiences during these months. As a diligent educator who is trying to complete the required course and grade-level requirements, it is easy to become focused on performance standards and forget that we are dealing with real people who need to have their personal lives validated in our curriculum in order to truly engage in the learning process (Garcia, 1994; Nieto, 2000; Sleeter & Grant, 1999). *Incorporate fun activities into your everyday lessons that will enhance the cultural connections you are trying to make with your diverse learners throughout the entire school year* (see Cech and Tiedt & Tiedt in Resource B, Recommended Reading).

After many years of teaching in all types and sizes of educational settings, I have discovered that teachers wear many hats—and one of them is that of a game show host! Don't be afraid to have fun with your students. Make the learning experience as lively and entertaining as possible while still honing in on the academic standards that must be met. Try to lure your students into learning through interesting, student-centered activities. And remember, as you continue to express excitement about the curriculum, that enthusiasm will be contagious!

APRIL TO JUNE: "HANG IN THERE, BABY!"

You may have seen the famous poster of a kitten clinging to a tree limb with its tiny claws. The expression on the whiskered face is a cross between great consternation and sheer terror, and the caption underneath says it all: *"Hang in There, Baby!"* This is exactly how many educators feel after Spring Break has ended. Often our students return from their vacation with renewed vitality and vigor, but their focus is far from the learning environment. Their minds are anticipating the approach of summer—you know, the sand, surf, and sun. Friends and fun are at the forefront of their interests, while some students can't get their thoughts off graduation. If you're lucky, there will be a few kids left who remember that school's still in session!

There's a strong chance that you can relate to their waning attention spans. It has been a long haul! If you think back to September and what has been accomplished since that time, you'll be amazed with the progress all of you have made this year. Together you've shuffled multitudes of papers back and forth, met school/district/state standards, and survived the ups and downs of the educational journey. In fact, you may be more ready for this vacation than your students are!

Well, "hang in there!" You are not alone. Many experienced teachers will tell you that even after many years in the classroom, they still feel this way. As a new educator who is just learning about this profession, you've probably expended more energy than you have in any other job. Some experts in this field even describe the adventure during the first year as "survival of the fittest" (Jensen & Kiley, 2000). You have a right to be a little worn down, but don't give in to these feelings! Also, don't take your pupils' malaise personally. Most of them still like you and your class, but they're tired—or perhaps they've simply lost their focus and need you to get them back on track for the final months of school.

This is the ideal time to have a "heart-to-heart" talk with your students. Basically this means sitting down and sharing what has been happening (or *not* happening) in the class. This technique is actually beneficial at any point during the school year when you sense your students could use a "reality check." Maybe grades are slipping. Perhaps homework isn't being turned in. It might be that you need to review class expectations because there have been some behavior problems. Share your concerns, and be sure to let them know that you can relate to how they may be feeling right now. Allow the students to have a chance to respond, and then see if you can work together to devise a plan for success during these final weeks of school. Student involvement in the decision-making process not only results in excellent ideas for the learning environment but also increases the likelihood of student cooperation (Jensen & Kiley, 2000; Weinstein, 1996).

Finding activities that stimulate your students is an important key to re-energizing bodies, minds, and spirits that may have temporarily shut down. Young people love projects in which they can work and learn together, especially if they can delve into their own areas of interest. Think of an exciting, enjoyable project for the last week or two of school that will tie together the academic principles that you want to stress but will also be memorable for the kids. Let the students share these in presentation form during the final days of school, maybe while snacking on popcorn and drinking sodas. Whatever you do, be sure that you end the year in some special way. As a wise administrator once told me, it's the fun stuff that the students will remember anyway!

YEAR-ROUND SCHOOL

As I mentioned earlier, many schools are no longer on the "traditional" calendar. There are a variety of reasons for this, one of which is fiscal. Many districts cannot afford to build new schools, so the utilization of current sites is essential. In order to get more students onto one campus, calendars are adjusted so that schools can have multiple schedules running all throughout the year. Another reason for the change from a September through June schedule is philosophical. For many regions, farms no longer need to be worked and harvested, so students can attend classes during summer months without it being a hardship on their families. Also, there are a number of educators who believe that shorter breaks between sessions allow for better retention of information as well as a consistent level of enthusiasm for learning.

You may know students and teachers who actually start the school year in July. They may have only one month for summer vacation, but every nine weeks at school are followed by a three-week break. Although these schedules can take some getting used to, there are many teachers, administrators, parents, and students who are thrilled with the overall aspects of year-round schools. If you are uncertain about the benefits of this type of educational calendar, talk to those who have been on this type of schedule to get more feedback.

No matter what type of schedule your school may follow, you will find that the ebbs and flows of the seasons are quite similar in most academic settings. Almost everyone begins the school year with a tremendous amount of excitement, especially you—the new educator! As the year progresses, the energy levels can drop; this is when the students might lose their focus and concentration. As the captain, leader, conductor, producer, artist, director, coach, manager, and even cheerleader of the classroom, it will be up to you to maintain the course set before you and keep everyone on the right track.

Tips to Remember

1. Talk to your fellow teachers about activities, projects, and programs to try at different points during the school year. They may have great ideas that you can integrate into your own curriculum.

2. Gather magazines, old calendars, catalogs, and other visuals that can be used to create seasonal bulletin boards. Let your students decorate the classroom with colorful pictures and posters that celebrate their cultures as well as those of other kids from around the globe!

3. Look through teacher supply catalogs and stores for seasonal workbooks that apply to your grade level or subject area. There are numerous multicultural materials that can be easily implemented in any educational setting.

4. Check with an administrator for stipulations on any end-of-the-year activities. For example, some may not want any field trips during the last few weeks of school, while others may require that a special event be either on or off campus because of graduation ceremonies. Whatever you do, have a memorable last day planned for you and your students!

1 1

Crossing the Finish Line

Time to Celebrate Your Success

Review, review, REVIEW, reproducing the old, deepening its impression with new thought, linking it with added meanings, finding new applications, correcting any false views, and completing the true.

—John Milton Gregory

"Congratulations on finishing your first year of teaching.
All of the other kindergarten teachers would like you to
have this gold watch—we made it ourselves
from ice cream sticks and glitter!"

Whether on foot or horseback, in a car or on a train, all adventurers know the pleasure of finally reaching the desired destination. And, following any arduous trip, these travelers are ready for some rest and relaxation after the trials and triumphs of their journey. For you, the professional teacher, this is the culmination of countless years of preparation. Perhaps you dreamed of becoming an educator since childhood. Maybe you left a secure position in order to seek out a profession that you always admired but didn't have the opportunity to explore earlier. So here you are—a year of teaching under your belt, and another exciting season with students awaiting you just around the corner.

THE LAST DAYS OF CLASS

The end of the school year should be a momentous occasion for you. Think back to where you were just 12 months ago. As you faithfully filled out application forms and prepared for the interview experience, you were probably also praying that the phone would ring before summer vacation ended! After that crucial call came, you put your best foot forward, and, before long, a contract awaited your signature. Then the real work started! You had to study the curriculum and standards, clean and organize your classroom, and set about establishing firm but fair behavioral and academic expectations. After this, the students arrived with all of their diverse abilities and needs. You stepped out together on the journey of learning with a sense of expectation and excitement energizing your efforts. Now, after an eventful year, your students are moving on, rich in the new knowledge and experiences that you imparted, and ready to meet the requirements of the next grade level.

Yes, you *have* accomplished a lot! If you're tired—or even totally exhausted—you've got a good reason for feeling this way! Not every job is as rigorous as teaching, and few require all of the responsibilities that you have undertaken. That's why I believe it is essential for educators to take time during their vacations to celebrate the successes of the school year, and simply to rest and relax for a season.

THE WELL-DESERVED RESPITE

Many professionals make the mistake of assuming they must continue to push ahead in their careers without taking a break. Unfortunately, in many cases these workers quickly grow weary from the stresses and strains of their jobs. You've probably known a family member or friend who simply "burned out" in his or her career and, either by choice or not, had to look for another job. Teachers can find themselves facing this same fate unless they learn early on how to really take care of themselves. *As you know, a marvelous aspect of this profession is the built-in breaks that occur throughout the school year.* This means that those of us in the field of education have no excuse for not resting and relaxing for a little while. In fact, many people are envious of the so-called easy schedule that teachers have. Well, after you've finished this draining first year of teaching, you've gained new insights as to why we have these respites!

Everyone's definition of rest varies, and your idea of taking a break may be quite different than your fellow staff members.' What matters most is that you do those things that allow you to let go of everyday pressures and concerns for a while and truly relax. If you're more at ease in your recliner chair, then sit in it for days until you feel ready to get up and go somewhere. If you're the type who will tinker and toil around the house if you stay put, then I'd recommend planning a trip out of town so you'll be forced to do nothing at all. Even if you don't have a lot of extra money (which most new professionals are often short on while they pay off student loans), you can always find inexpensive getaways not too far from home. The point is that you should try to see some new scenery and break out of your everyday routine!

Speaking of travel, many teachers have discovered that this is a wonderful pastime during their summer vacation or long breaks. Actually, traveling is the optimum method for learning about our world. You actually see (visual), hear (auditory), and experience (kinesthetic) the information while you're on the journey. Not only will your trip create lasting memories, but it will also open your eyes to the diversity of people and cultures in our world. If money is a concern, then set up a special account just for these jaunts. Even $50 a month will give you a small sum to spend on a short expedition to someplace special.

Remember that many types of traveling experiences can become part of your professional development plan (the PDP that we discussed in Chapter 9). Check with your state commission on teacher credentialing for the particular guidelines about travel and be sure to keep detailed records of dates, places, and activities that you experienced. For example, if you attend a play in a particular country, keep the ticket stub and program, and jot some notes so that you can remember any specific things that you gleaned from the performance. Later, you can fill these items in on your PDP form, plus complete any other requirements that your state guidelines may suggest. For instance, you may be asked to write a short essay about your visit and attach this to your PDP for review.

Whatever you do, be sure to make the effort during these built-in breaks to pamper yourself personally. Do things that you enjoy, even if it is simply taking a bike ride, playing golf, or having lunch with a friend. If something sounds fun, it should be at the top of any "to do" list for this vacation. And, don't let guilt slip its way into your thoughts; you've earned the right to take time off, and your new students will benefit from having a teacher who's totally refreshed and reenergized!

REFLECTION

During the student teaching process, your university supervisor should have asked you to do some form of reflective exercises on your interactions in the classroom. You may have written down thoughts in a journal or simply discussed with him or her how you think things went. The purpose of this type of exercise is to give you the opportunity to consider what things went well—and what didn't go exactly as you hoped (Jensen & Kiley, 2000). Reflection—the ability to step outside of our personal circumstances—is also part of the metacognitive skills we hope to instill in our own students (Banks, 1994). As you consciously review the way that the students responded to the curriculum as well as your presentation methods, you will become more cognizant of ways to improve the experiences in your classroom.

This is also an important process to undertake while you are on vacation. After you have rested and relaxed for a few days, or even several weeks, take a notebook or journal to a quiet place—perhaps your favorite park or coffee shop—and start thinking back to the beginning of the school year. What opening activities really set a nice atmosphere for your students? Were there ways you could have improved the connections you made with kids earlier than you did? What about the curriculum? Are there weaknesses that you should spend some time working on? Did you feel that your content corresponded with the achievement results on the standardized testing? Perhaps you can search for materials that will improve overall instruction as well as make more cultural connections in your classroom. Mentally walk through the year, step by step, making notes on all of the positive aspects as well as anything that definitely needs improvement.

The reason why I recommend you write these things down is twofold: 1. You'll have a record of your successes from this first year of teaching, and 2. You'll know exactly what areas to improve upon for next year. But just thinking about these things is not enough; you must formulate a plan. After a few days have passed, look over your ideas again. Finally, create a separate list of things you can focus on during your vacation that will really add depth and meaning to your second year of teaching. Some of these items may become part of the goals you set for your professional development plan.

By the way, this process doesn't mean that the fun, surf, sun, sleeping in, tennis, and trips have to end! You need to maintain that restful vacation mode, but you'll find that once you've gotten these things off your mind and onto paper, you'll be able to relax even more. It's similar to having your grocery list floating around in your head; these thoughts can be so annoying, especially as you attempt *not* to forget something. Once you finally grab a notepad and write them down, all of a sudden your mind is able to let those matters go because you know that you've got them safe and secure for future reference.

As your vacation passes, spend some time considering methods to enhance your instructional techniques and curriculum for next year. On occasion, review your list, and add new ideas that pop into your head. Often as we travel, get together with friends, see movies, or read books, we'll get brainstorms about how to make our classes even better. If you find resources that would be positive additions to your curriculum, think about purchasing them or adding them to your wish list for the school to order. Most important, concentrate on all the things that went well this year so that you can celebrate the successes that you had with your students!

READ, AND GET READY!

I've never met a teacher who doesn't like reading. I guess that's part of the reason that we've all been drawn to this profession: There's some inner urging for and attraction to the written word. The only problem is that once educators take control of their own classrooms, they seldom have time to enjoy their own types of books. Most of the school year is spent looking over new learning materials, educational journals, or mandatory documents, as well as keeping up on the information that must be presented to the students!

This leads us to yet another benefit of vacations and other breaks for teachers—you can read to your heart's content! This might mean picking up that novel that's been gathering dust on the nightstand, or finding a fascinating piece of nonfiction that's on the bestseller list. Maybe you have absolutely no idea what you'd like to peruse, so a trip to a local bookstore or library may be in order.

You should definitely spend some of your vacation getting lost in great literature. Not only is it a wonderful form of relaxation, but reading also keeps your mind active and alert, which is a necessity in this profession! In addition, if you truly want to teach students how to be lifelong learners, then you must exercise and exhibit those habits in your own life (Jensen & Kiley, 2000; Wong & Wong, 1998). I would also suggest that you look over the list I have provided for you in Resource B, Recommended Reading. These books are among the best I have found for educators, so selecting one or two a year to review would be an asset to your professional expertise. And don't forget to keep an eye out for any current materials related to your credential or specialty area.

As you sip some iced tea and slip away to read your novel, you'll automatically be getting the rest and reflection time you need to prepare for the upcoming school year. When you are relaxed and reenergized, you'll be more than ready to meet the challenges of your new students. Begin to envision what the next group of diverse learners will be like, and start to gear up for the exciting times that lie ahead.

You have joined the ranks of a prestigious group of professionals—those who have chosen to dedicate their hearts, souls, and minds to the lives of our greatest resource—children. As many educators will tell you, the path you have chosen will not be an easy one. You will have tough days and long nights. You'll experience people with short fuses and lots of excuses. Sometimes everything will run smoothly, and other times you'll wonder what ever happened to the plans you made! You may even feel discouraged or depressed at times—but don't despair! Everyone, and I mean *everyone*, feels this way at some point in his or her career. It's part of the human experience to get exasperated and exhausted from time to time. Remember, "Hang in there, baby!" These feelings won't last forever.

What *will* last is the memory of the smile on the student's face when he finally understands a lesson, or the note that a quiet child slips on your desk to say thank you for caring. You'll treasure the hugs and high fives forever, and no amount of money can buy that blessed phrase, *"You're the best teacher that I've ever had!"* Even now, these memories from my own experiences with students bring tears to my eyes.

What an incredible adventure lies ahead of you! The journey you've set out on will take you through many seasons and shifts in educational thought and theory. It will be filled with new people, places, and potential. Although you may still feel a little unsteady, you've successfully taken those first few strides into this exciting profession. Use all the tools, tricks, and techniques that you've tucked in your teaching backpack, and keep gathering up new ideas and innovations as you come across them. After all of the time, energy, and effort that you've put forth this year, you'll be able to step into your new career with confidence and truly enjoy every aspect of the amazing days that await you—not only during the first days of class, but all the way along your journey in education!

Tips to Remember

1. Keep a scrapbook of notes, cards, and photos from each year of teaching to help you remember who was who. This way you can reflect on all the great times that you've spent with your students—especially on days when you're feeling a little low or aren't sure if you're making a difference in the world.

2. Check into travel opportunities that are offered to teachers. Look for funding from research organizations like the National Endowment for the Humanities (NEH) and Fulbright. Some districts have special group activities, and many travel agencies will be aware of package deals that may be very affordable for an educator's budget.

3. Write notes to the principal and staff members to thank them for the support they've given you this year.

4. If you feel it's the right timing, ask key people for letters of recommendation so you can add them to your placement file. Be sure to provide a pre-addressed, stamped envelope and any special form your university requires for this process.

RESOURCE A

A TEACHER'S TEN COMMANDMENTS

1. Seek advice. No one is an expert at everything.

2. Get organized!

3. Be aware of each child's needs.

4. Plan ahead.

5. Be flexible—changes are inevitable.

6. Stay in touch with parents; they are your vital link!

7. Read, read, READ!

8. Keep teaching as long as you enjoy it.

9. Act professionally. Your position is as important to our society as that of a doctor, banker, lawyer, or businessperson!

10. Remember, you ARE making a difference in the world!

—Rebecca Lynn Wilke, Ed.D.

RESOURCE B

RECOMMENDED READING

Although you will have much to do during your first year of teaching, you may be able to squeeze in some time for a few of these essential reads. Summers are also ideal times to catch up on the classics of your profession.

Armstrong, T. (1998). *Awakening Genius in the Classroom.* Alexandria, VA: Association for Supervision and Curriculum Development.

Banks, J. A. (1997). *Teaching Strategies for Ethnic Studies* (3rd ed.). Boston: Allyn & Bacon.

Cech, M. (1991). *Globalchild: Multicultural Resources for Young Children.* Menlo Park, CA: Addison-Wesley.

Codell, E. R., & Trelease, J. (1999). *Educating Esme: Diary of a Teacher's First Year.* Chapel Hill, NC: Algonquin Books.

Cole, R. W. (Ed.). (1995). *Educating Everybody's Children: Diverse Teaching Strategies for Diverse Learners.* Arlington, VA: Association for Supervision and Curriculum Development.

Covey, S. R. (1990). *The 7 Habits of Highly Effective People: Powerful Lessons in Personal Change.* New York: Fireside.

Curwin, R. L., & Mandler, A. N. (1988). *Discipline With Dignity.* Alexandria, VA: Association for Supervision and Curriculum Development.

DeRoche, E. F., & Williams, M. M. (1998). *Educating Hearts and Minds: A Comprehensive Character Education Framework.* Thousand Oaks, CA: Corwin.

Freire, P. (1997). *Pedagogy of the Oppressed.* New York: The Continuum.

Goodlad, J. I. (1984). *A Place Called School: Prospects for the Future.* New York: McGraw-Hill.

Green, L. (1986). *Kids Who Underachieve.* New York: Simon and Schuster.

Howard, G. R. (1999). *We Can't Teach What We Don't Know: White Teachers, Multiracial Schools.* New York: Teachers College Press.

Jenson, R. (1995). *Make a Life, Not Just a Living: 10 Timeless Life Skills That Will Maximize Your Real Net Worth.* Nashville, TN: Broadman & Holman.

Krashen, S. (1981). *Second Language Acquisition and Second Language Learning.* New York: Pergamon.

Krashen, S., & Terrell, T. (1983). *The Natural Approach: Language Acquisition in the Classroom.* Hayward, CA: Alemany Press.

Lindfors, J. W. (1999). *Children's Inquiry: Using Language to Make Sense of The World.* New York: Teachers College Press.

Maker, C. J., & King, M. A. (1996). *Nurturing Giftedness in Young Children.* Reston, VA: Council for Exceptional Children.

Peddiwell, J. A. (1939). *The Saber-Tooth Curriculum.* New York: McGraw-Hill.

Sizer, T. (1984). *Horace's Compromise: The Dilemma of the American High School.* Boston: Houghton Mifflin.

Takaki, R. (1993). *A Different Mirror: A History of Multicultural America.* Boston: Little, Brown.

Tiedt, P. L., & Tiedt, I. M. (1999). *Multicultural Teaching: A Handbook of Activities, Information, and Resources, 5th Edition.* Boston: Allyn & Bacon.

Trelease, J. (1987). *The Read-Aloud Handbook.* Victoria, Australia: Penguin Books.

RESOURCE C

WEB SITES

Professional Web Sites

http://www.nces.ed.gov
   The National Center for Educational Statistics offers up-to-date information for educators on important issues as well as national testing results and statistics.

http://www.ed.gov
   The U.S. Department of Education's site contains a wealth of data supporting its goal to "provide educational excellence for all Americans."

http://www.aft.org
   The American Federation of Teacher's (AFT) provides information on political issues and other pertinent topics that is of great interest to many in the profession.

http://www.nea.org
   This site for the National Education Association includes details on membership, current topics in education, and free educational materials.

http://www.ericsp.org
   The Educational Resource Information Center (ERIC) offers links to a variety of other sites to find material related to your particular area of interest.

Practical Web Sites

http://www.discovery.com

The Discovery Channel's site covers interesting subjects like astronomy, history, and health. A current list of their television shows is also available.

http://www.pbs.org

Everything from the arts to politics can be found on PBS Online. The PBS kids section is colorful and interactive.

http://www.scholastic.com

Scholastic Inc. offers educational information for teachers, parents, and kids. Classroom lessons and activities as well as resources are located here.

http://www.thehistorynet.com

The History Place has current as well as archived information on just about anything a classroom teacher would want to know. Events and exhibits as well as an article index are available.

http://www.nationalgeographic.com

Great photography and articles abound at this world-renowned magazine's site. Interactive features would be useful in the classroom.

http://www.cnn.com

Breaking news and current global issues are available at the click of your mouse. There are links to good articles in the field of education as well.

http://www.classroom.com

Classroom Connect links classroom teachers via the Internet while providing a variety of resources and ideas.

http://exploratorium.edu

San Francisco's famous Exploratorium offers this site as a museum of "science, art, and human perception." A digital library provides images, archived Webcasts, and search capabilities.

Multicultural Web Sites

http://www.nmci.org

The National Multicultural Institute offers information on diversity training, conferences, and NMCI publications.

http://www.estrellita.com

Bilingual Education Resources in Spanish are available as well as updates on conferences across the United States.

http://www.iteachnet.com/webmulticultural.html

Web resources for multicultural issues that will be of interest to the classroom teacher are available here.

References

Armstrong, T. (2000). *Multiple intelligences in the classroom* (2nd ed.). Alexandria, VA: Association for Supervision and Curriculum Development.

Banks, J. A. (1994). *Multiethnic education: Theory and practice* (3rd ed.). Boston: Allyn & Bacon.

Curwin, R. L., & Mendler, A. N. (1999). *Discipline with dignity.* Alexandria, VA: Association for Supervision and Curriculum Development.

Darling-Hammond, L. (1997). *The right to learn: A blueprint for creating schools that work.* San Francisco: Jossey-Bass.

Darling-Hammond, L., Berry, B. T., Haselkorn, D., & Fideler, E. (1999). Teacher recruitment, selection, and induction: Policy influences on the supply and quality of teachers. In L. Darling-Hammond and G. Sykes (Eds.), *Teaching as the learning profession: Handbook of policy and practice.* San Francisco: Jossey-Bass.

Deal, T. E., & Kennedy, A. A. (1982). *Corporate cultures: The rites and rituals of corporate life.* New York: Addison-Wesley.

DeRoche, E. F., & Williams, M. M. (2001). *Educating hearts and minds: A comprehensive character education framework.* Thousand Oaks, CA: Corwin.

Fideler, E., & Haselkorn, D. (1999). *Learning the ropes: Urban teacher induction programs and practices in the United States.* Belmont, MA: Recruiting New Teachers.

Fullan, M. (1993). *Change forces: Probing the depths of educational reform.* New York: The Falmer Press.

Garcia, E. (1994). *Understanding and meeting the challenge of student cultural diversity.* Boston: Houghton Mifflin.

Gardner, H. (1993). *Multiple intelligences: The theory in practice.* New York: Basic Books.

Gardner, H. (2000). *Intelligence reframed: Multiple intelligences for the 21st century.* New York: Basic Books.

Gregory, J. M. (1954). *The seven laws of teaching*. Grand Rapids, MI: Baker Book House.

Humes, J. C. (1978). *Speaker's treasury of anecdotes about the famous*. New York: Harper and Row.

Jensen, R. A., & Kiley, T. J. (2000). *Teaching, leading, and learning: Becoming caring professionals*. Boston: Houghton Mifflin.

Johnson, D. W., Johnson, R. T., & Holubec, E. J. (1994). *Cooperative learning in the classroom*. Alexandria, VA: Association for Supervision and Curriculum Development.

Johnson, J. A., Dupuis, V. L., Musial, D., Hall, G. E., & Gollnick, D. M. (2002). *Introduction to the foundations of American education* (12th ed.). Boston: Allyn & Bacon.

Krashen, S. (1981). *Second language acquisition and second language learning*. New York: Pergamon.

Lee, D. (Trans.). (1987). *Plato: The Republic*. New York: Penguin Books.

Lyons, N. (Ed.). (1998). *With portfolio in hand: Validating the new teacher professionalism*. New York: Teachers College Press.

McGinnis, A. L. (1985). *Bringing out the best in people*. Minneapolis, MN: Augsburg.

McNeil, J. (1996). *Curriculum: A comprehensive introduction* (5th ed.). New York: HarperCollins.

National Association of Independent Schools. *Fact Sheet*. (October 2000). Retrieved November 1, 2000, from www.nais.org/nais/nafact.html

National Center for Education Statistics. *Digest of Education Statistics, 1999* (chap. 2). Retrieved October 1, 2000, from www.nces.ed.gov/pubs2000/digest99

National Education Association Handbook. (1971–1972). Washington, DC: The Association.

Nieto, S. (2000). *Affirming diversity: The sociopolitical context of multicultural education* (3rd ed.). New York: Longman.

Noel, J. (2000). *Notable selections in multicultural education*. Guilford, CT: Dushkin/McGraw-Hill.

Pellicer, L. O., & Anderson, L. W. (1995). *A handbook for teacher leaders*. Thousand Oaks, CA: Corwin.

Shatzer, V. (1999). *History of American education: From Harvard scholars to worker bees of the new world order*. Oklahoma City, OK: Heartstone.

Shea, T. M., & Bauer, A. M. (1997). *An introduction to special education: A social systems perspective.* Chicago: Brown & Benchmark.

Sleeter, C. E., & Grant, C. A. (1999). *Making choices for multicultural education: Five approaches to race, class, and gender* (3rd ed.). New York: John Wiley & Sons.

Smith, T. E. C., Polloway, E. A., Patton, J. R., & Dowdy, C. A. (1998). *Teaching students with special needs in inclusive settings* (2nd ed.). Boston: Allyn & Bacon.

Spring, J. (2002). *American education* (10th ed.). Boston: McGraw-Hill.

Wehman, P. (1997). *Exceptional individuals in school, community, and work.* Austin, TX: Pro-ed.

Weinstein, C. S. (1996). *Secondary classroom management.* Boston: McGraw-Hill.

Wilke, R. L. (1997). *A multicultural curriculum's relationships to attitudes of prejudice and stereotyping in 5th and 6th grade students.* Unpublished doctoral dissertation, University of Southern California.

Wong, H. K., & Wong, R. T. (1998). *The first days of school: How to be an effective teacher* (2nd ed.). Mountain View, CA: Harry K. Wong.

Index

Professional teaching portfolio,
11-13, 14
Public schools, 9

Resume, professional, 10-11, 14
posting online, 11
what to include, 10-11
Rewards:
for good behavior, 61
for good citizenship, 61
Rubrics, 70-71, 72
report cards and, 71
student-designed, 71

Salaries, 6
Scholastic Inc. Web site, 120
School administrators, 79-80. *See also*
Assistant principals; Principals;
Superintendents
School crisis plans, 53
School culture, 16-17, 80
environment, 16
heroes, 16
negative aspects, 17
positive aspects, 17
rites and rituals, 16
taking notes on, 22
values, 16
See also Culture bearers
School map, 53
Schools, types of, 9-10
parochial, 9
private, 9
public, 9
School year cycle, 98-99
April to June, 103-104
end-of-year activities, 106
January to March, 100, 102-103
October to December, 99-100
year-round school and, 104-105
See also Curriculum
Scrapbook, keeping teaching, 114
Self-assessment, 3-6
cultural heritage, 5-6
intelligence type, 4-5
learning style, 4
See also Self-reflection

Self-reflection, 3-4
daily, 63
first day of school, 63
pre-teaching interview, 2-3
See also Self-assessment
Shatzer, V., 9
Shea, T. M., 47, 48, 49
Sleeter, C. E., 44, 102
Smith, T. E. C., 47, 48
Special needs students, 47-49. *See also*
Attention-deficit/Hyperactivity
Disorder (ADHD); Individualized
Education Plans (IEPs); Learning
disabilities
Spring, J., 9, 25, 43, 44, 67, 89, 92, 93
Standardized testing:
accountability and, 25
schedule, 25
Standards:
district, 67
school, 67
state, 67
subject content and, 67
Students:
assessing ability levels of, 46
assessing learning styles of, 46-47
assessing prior knowledge
of, 45-46
as unique individuals, 43, 49
first impressions of teacher, 42
linguistically diverse, 44
reviewing diagnostic data on, 46
teacher's importance in lives of, 57
with special gifts/talents, 68
See also Culturally diverse learners;
Learning disabled students;
Special needs students
Substitute plans, school policy
concerning, 40
Superintendents, 79

Teacher Appreciation Day, 58
Teachers:
as authority figures, 64
as power brokers, 67
demand for, xi
importance in lives of students, 57

**CORWIN
PRESS**

The Corwin Press logo—a raven striding across an open book—represents the happy union of courage and learning. We are a professional-level publisher of books and journals for K-12 educators, and we are committed to creating and providing resources that embody these qualities. Corwin's motto is "Success for All Learners."